The Prepper's Handbook
Second Edition

Don't be scared
Don't panic
Just prepare

By

Bryan Foster, aka Zion Prepper
&
Camden Foster, aka Zion Prepper Jr.

Contents

Introduction

When I originally wrote *The Prepper's Handbook* I had no idea the journey I had begun. It would ultimately determine what I wanted to do in life. My goal was to capture my prepper experience and knowledge and pass it on. I had no idea that others were on a similar journey, or even more surprising, interested in my journey. In my wildest dreams I had no idea that I would enjoy writing books; after all, in college I had to take English 101 five times before I passed. I had no experience or knowledge in how to create a book cover or format the interior of a book. I had no background in marketing or social media. These are things I have learned and look forward to as I continue my writings. My greatest accomplishment is the impact that my writings and hands-on prepping experience has had on my youngest son. Not only does he actively participate in prepping but he, too, has begun to write his first book. My dream is that one day he will continue to update and expand my writings. I'm excited for him and love watching him develop and find his own future.

Today I'm proud to bring you the second edition of *The Prepper's Handbook*. This updated version of *The Prepper's Handbook* will cover the original material I wrote but also include much more. *The Prepper's Handbook* has been completely updated and revised with significantly more new material. This updated version of *The Prepper's Handbook* will provide and explore techniques (skills) and recommendations within the context of The Survival Triangle©, Ten Commandments of Prepping, and Five Tenets of Prepping. If you have not read my books before you will find that I believe that the premise for successful prepping is The Survival Triangle©. The Survival Triangle© is a model outlining the requirements for a balanced approach to prepping, while the Ten Commandments of Prepping provides a guiding belief of the prepper lifestyle. The Five Tenets of Prepping provides the framework, understanding, and importance of traditional and nontraditional techniques and recommendations.

In the first edition of *The Prepper's Handbook* I provided many high-level concepts and through time realized that my readers wanted more detail. In addition, as my experience, knowledge, and relationships have grown, I also realized that I needed to redefine who and what a prepper is as well as the prepper lifestyle. As a result, this edition of *The Prepper's Handbook* will provide a more detailed look at the prepper and prepper lifestyle. I have expanded the original Four Tenets of Prepping to include a fifth tenet and added the Ten Commandments of Prepping. Finally, I have included a detailed understanding of prepper vocabulary to include many commonly used words and terms, such as bug-out bag, shit hits the fan (SHTF), bug-out location, the end of the world as we know it (TEOTWAWKI), and without rule of law (WROL), to name a few.

I will describe recommendations that provide general suggestions as well as an alternative viewpoint of the prepper philosophy. This is an important concept because in a Significant Life Altering Event (SLAE) or Shit Hits The Fan (SHTF) scenario, our "traditional" lifestyle will be forever changed. There exists the potential to no longer have electricity, running water, grocery stores, hospitals, or even the infrastructure we rely on today. As preppers it's incumbent that we are open to and learn new ideas, techniques, and recommendations. We will be required to adapt and overcome while using resources traditionally not used. Throughout this book I will refer to these techniques and recommendations as "tools." These tools become extremely important when you consider that you can only live:

- three seconds without the desire to live
- three minutes without air
- three hours without shelter or fire

- three days without water
- three weeks without food
- three months without hope for the future

Though mainstream survival and prepper techniques are extremely important, there are many times non-traditional techniques or methods will provide similar if not the same result and success or these techniques may be the only option available. You won't necessarily find these non-traditional tools in the mainstream prepping community, and many of them you may never have heard of before. These tools are often passed down from generation to generation. Some of these tools will be true and time-tested, while others are recently learned. Several will be relatively unknown or even rarely communicated. They are used or created by everyday people, many of whom don't consider themselves a prepper or even know the term. These everyday people can range from those living in the backwoods of the Smoky Mountains to the family that lives off-grid to city dwellers. For some there is no other way of life but to use these tools. As such I will include both traditional and non-traditional understandings throughout this handbook. In other words, I provide the guidance and you chose the best option that works for you.

To provide a well-rounded understanding, I share my experience and knowledge, as well as that of experts within the prepper and survivalist community. Where I find I'm not an expert or have limited experience, I describe verbatim understanding and recommendations from those who are experts.

I present the information just as others have shared and instructed me. What you will be exposed to here may only be practical in certain or limited situations, but nevertheless it could save your life one day. In essence, the tools I present offer practicality as well as functionality during a Shit Hits the Fan (SHTF) or Significant Life-Altering Event (SLAE) scenario. Once again, as the author, my sole purpose is to expose you, the reader, to an overview of prepping within the context of The Survival Triangle©, Ten Commandments of Prepping, and Five Tenets of Prepping. Many of the recommendations presented will here require follow-up and practice by you. I present the concepts in order to allow you to determine the practicality of the skill or recommendation in your particular situation. Many will appreciate the general overview, while others will study the various subjects in much more detail.

If you are a survivalist or homesteader, this handbook will provide value but it's most practical to those who

want to understand prepping based on the most
common scenario. That scenario is:

- you want to be prepared to shelter-in-place
  between seventy-two hours and twelve months.
- you have neighbors and live in a town or city.
- you rely on city or town water, electricity, and
  sewage.
- you understand that in a Significant Life Altering
  Event (SLAE) stores will quickly run out or not
  have access to the staples (food, water, bread,
  etc.).
- you're open-minded and understand that you
  can't predict when you may be required to
  shelter-in-place or rely on your preparations.
- you want to provide a safe, comfortable
  environment for yourself, family or group during
  a SLAE event.

As sad as it is, I have to give a legal disclaimer. As you
read through this guide, please understand that it is
intended for educational purposes only. My statements
should not be used as, or in place of, medical or survival
advice. I have communicated with experts and
conducted extensive research on the topics in this guide
and I have had personal experience with the
information I present. I consider myself a professional

and well-versed in numerous subjects, which includes prepping, but do your own research and create your own experiences. I provide this information strictly for your reference and consideration.

Bryan and Camden Foster

The Prepper's Handbook – Second Edition

Definitions

Before we begin let's review the definitions of terms used throughout this book as well as in the prepper community.

- Black-Out Bag: A backpack or other portable storage device that contains electrical or electrical-related items. Because of the portability of the Black-Out Bag it can be used at your primary shelter or transported to an alternate location. The contents of the Black-Out Bag are used during a temporary loss of power lasting no more than two weeks. Items include:
  - ○ Deep-cycle batteries connected either in series or parallel. This will be your power (energy) source.

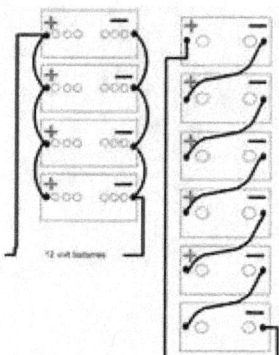

Diagram of 12-volt batteries in parallel and series configurations

o   Inverters: convert direct current (DC), which in this case is provided by deep-cycle batteries, into alternating current (AC). Alternating current is what you use in your house when you plug something into an outlet. Basically, when electricity is not available, deep-cycle batteries allow you to power a limited number of electrical items based on wattage and the rating of the battery. As you use the inverter and deep-cycle batteries to power electrical items, the batteries must be recharged. Inverters typically range in size from 150 watts to well over 10,000 watts.

12-volt Radio Shack™ inverter

o   Power strip to connect directly to the inverter.
o   Electrical wire/wire caps of different gauges.
o   Electrical, duck, and shrink tape.

- o Plastic wire ties.
- o Adapters for smart phones, USB connections,
- o Multi-prong 12v adapter.
  - Plugs into the cigarette lighter to give you two 12-volt receptacles.

Multi-prong 12-volt adapter

- o 12-volt accessories such as LED lights, phone/electronic chargers, portable air compressor, GPS, small portable coolers, and even power tools.

- Bug In: A scenario in which you stay at your current location and rely on existing preparations and resources for sustainability. Typically a bug-in location is a primary residence, apartment, trailer, or other long-term housing. More often than not families will shelter-in-place at their primary shelter.

- Bug Out: A scenario in which a prepper has evaluated his/her surroundings and determined that it's no longer safe to remain at that location because of man-made or natural disasters. The prepper heads or "bugs out" to a predetermined location to ensure the safety of the individual, family or group.

- Bug-Out Bag (BOB) or Go Bag: A backpack or other portable pack that contains items necessary to survive, on average, from twenty-four to seventy-two hours. A BOB is always ready to be utilized and is stored in a location with easy access and typically in the same location as a medical bug-out bag (MBOB). Examples of items found in a BOB include water, first aid kit, matches, flashlight, headlamp, food (typically dehydrated or freeze-dried), toiletries, extra set of clothing, personal medications, a means of communication (cell phone, portable radio, etc.), feminine hygiene products, matches, lighter, personal documents, multiple types of knives, spare batteries, extra cash or precious metal ingots (silver/gold), and fire starters, to name a few.

Bug-Out Bag (courtesy of USAMM's prepacked Bug-Out Bag)

Doggie Bug-Out Bag – Courtesy of prepforshtf.com
(For Doggie Bug out Bag details see: http://prepforshtf.com/wp-content/uploads/2012/12/Doggie_Bug_Out_LG.jpg)

- Bug-Out Location: A scenario in which you have evaluated your surroundings and determined that it's no longer safe to remain at that location because of man-made or natural disasters occurs. You then head or "bug out" to a predetermined location to ensure the safety of yourself, family or group.

Bug-Out Location

- Bug-Out Vehicle: Any transportation means utilized to relocate to an alternate location. Bug-out vehicles can include a truck, car, boat, recreational vehicle, motorcycle, airplane, and even an armored tank.

Bug-Out Vehicle (courtesy of http://www.tinypallethouse.com)

- Communications Bug-Out Bag: A backpack or other portable pack that contains communication gear to allow for the receiving and transmitting of information. Examples of communication gear include: portable weather radios, shortwave radio, Multi-Use Radio Service (MURS), Citizen Band (CB), General Mobile Radio Service (GMRS), ham radios, and computers.

- Medical Bug-Out Bag (MBOB): A backpack, first aid kit, or other portable pack that is dedicated to the storage of first aid supplies. A MBOB is always ready to be utilized, even in non-emergency situations, and is stored in a location with easy access. MBOBs are best stored in the same location as a bug-out bag.

  What a MBOB contains, as well as how much it carries, is determined by individual health, age, and the number of family members. Larger families may have multiple MBOBs.

- Get out of Dodge (GOOD): See "Bug Out"

- Preparations or Preps: Any item, physical or non-physical, used by the prepper to maximize survival in a shit hits the fan (SHTF) or significant life-altering event (SLAE) scenario. Items include: knowledge, experience, food, water, shelter, equipment, and community.

- Primary Shelter: A primary residence that you rely on for shelter. This is most often where you live on a day to day basis such as a house, trailer, apartment or condominium.

- Shelter-In-Place: See "Bug In."
  - o Sheltering-in-place is triggered by natural or man-made events that pose or will pose imminent danger.

- Shit Hits the Fan (SHTF): A significant event in which humanity as we know is forever changed. Preppers often use this acronym to describe a dire situation in which individuals, families or groups must be or become self-reliant. In most situations, preppers using this term assume that humanity is permanently affected and, once again, life as we know it will no longer be the same. Individuals not part of a prepper family or group are often not welcome and may be turned away. Examples of events associated with a SHTF scenario include: martial law, economic collapse, government actions (melt down), nuclear war, loss of the power grid, and coronal mass ejections. Words associated with a SHTF include: WROL (w̲ithout r̲ule o̲f l̲aw), TEOTWAWKI (t̲he e̲nd o̲f t̲he w̲orld a̲s w̲e k̲now i̲t), and BO (bug out).

- Significant Life-Altering Event (SLAE): A significant event that takes place in which an individual, group or organization is affected. Unlike a SHTF situation, a SLAE does not necessarily have an impact on all of humanity, although it may. In addition, the events of a SLAE can be personal in nature, not necessarily caused by mankind or nature, and can be temporary or permanent, dependent on circumstances. Examples of events associated with a SLAE include: death of a family member, loss of a job, coronal mass ejection, government collapse, and tornado.

Note: In both a SHTF and SLAE scenario, a prepper relies on prior planning and stored preparations. The difference between a SHTF and SLAE is who is affected (an individual, family, group or humanity) and the intensity of the event (localized earthquake, loss of job, martial law, economic collapse, etc.). Throughout this book I will use the

*acronyms SLAE and SHTF interchangeably, with each
simply meaning a life-altering event.*

- Stores: Any physical item used by the prepper to maximize survival in a SHTF or SLAE scenario. Examples include: food, water, heat, shelter, and protection.

- Survival Triangle: A model demonstrating the requirements, balance, and interdependence needed for proper prepping and survival. Furthermore, each element of The Survival Triangle© is supported by experience. This model will be defined in detail later in this book.

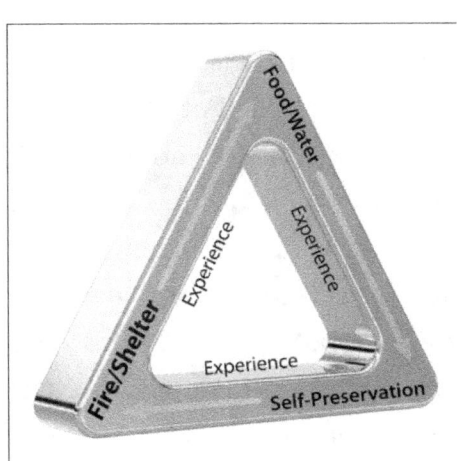

The Survival Triangle©

- The End of the World As We Know It (TEOTWAWKI): Preppers often use this term to describe a significant event that changes an individual, group or even humanity in a manner that significantly and negatively impairs one's way of life. A TEOTWAWKI, by the author's definition, can be either a SHTF or SLAE scenario. A TEOTWAWKI can be the loss of a job for one individual, while an economic collapse for another.

- Tools: Non-traditional ideas, techniques, and recommendations practiced prior to and used in a SHTF or SLAE.

- Without Rule of Law (WROL): An outcome that arises as a direct result of a SHTF or SLAE scenario. According to Almond, "WROL describes a possible future scenario in which one cannot count on law enforcement to enforce the law and protect citizens and their property. In the typical hypothetical WROL scenario, it is appropriate for one to don his (or her) tactical gear (w/mags, water and 1st aid kit) and rifle in order to defend against looters and violent gangs roaming around in desperation...or whatever the threat may be." Almond (2010)

What is a Prepper

To start, a good question to ask is, "Why use the word *prepper* instead of *homesteader* or *survivalist*?" I use *Prepper* to identify myself as an individual who is learning, teaching, and communicating skills and experiences that allow my family, as well as others, to prepare for events that may change society as we know it. When I talk with friends, as well as other preppers, and mention *survivalist*, the "lone wolf" mentality immediately comes to mind. First and foremost, by definition I am not a survivalist, and second, as a professional who wants to keep his job, I would never call myself a survivalist—right or wrong. Society has become cautious and sensitive to those who call themselves *survivalists*. Please understand I am *not* making judgments; I am simply sharing my experiences and interactions with those who call themselves survivalists.

When I mention the word *homesteader*, my peers think of *Little House on the Prairie*; they're not far off. A homesteader lives a simple, off-grid life. I don't live off-grid, and I'm not ready to live off-grid. To me, prepper is today's buzzword for a person who is not a survivalist, lone wolf or homesteader. A prepper is part survivalist and part homesteader. As previously described, most preppers live in a community (neighborhood) and rely on county, city, or state infrastructure services.

Calling myself a prepper has stimulated conversations with people who aren't familiar with the term. I've learned there are many individuals who are interested in prepping or consider themselves preppers, but don't reach out to other preppers due to perception. The vast majority of people I've met are non-judgmental and more interested in what and who a prepper is. RiverWalker, a fellow member of the prepper community, defines a prepper as:

> *"Prepper (noun): An individual or group that prepares or makes preparations in advance of, or prior to, any change in normal circumstances or lifestyle without significant reliance on other persons (i.e., being self-reliant), or without substantial assistance from outside resources (govt., etc.) in order to minimize the effects of that change on their current lifestyle."* (RiverWalker, 2010)

Nowhere in the definition does RiverWalker mention guns and ammunition. We must dismiss the general consensus that preppers are individuals who only collect guns and ammunition. As you will learn, I support and argue that a successful prepper understands The Survival Triangle© and uses that knowledge to take a balanced approach to prepping, not just guns and ammunition. Remember, prepping is a philosophy that must be understood, taught, and practiced in order to maximize survival in a Significant Life Altering Event (SLAE) or Shit Hits The Fan (SHTF) scenario. Because of this importance, I will explain in detail the philosophy by which most preppers live. From this information it is my hope that you, the reader, have a much better understanding of the importance of being prepared for unknown events or outcomes.

Being a prepper is not limited by location, mindset, or even the experience you have. Prepping is only limited by what you're willing to hear, learn, and apply to your life. Just as you purchased this book to learn more about prepping, it's fair to state that while many topics are beneficial to you while others are not. You will pick and chose what techniques and recommendations will work for you and your family. The goal is to then apply them to your life and perhaps pass those skills on to future generations. New preppers, as well as experienced preppers, must remember to respect the skills, knowledge, and lifestyle that each individual brings.

This allows you to be open to and share new skills and experiences.

Understand that prepping is a philosophy that maximizes survival in a number of scenarios, including short- and long-term events. Examples of short-term events include the loss of your job, temporary loss of power, earthquake, tornado, or snow storm. Examples of a long-term event can include the loss of the nation's infrastructure (electricity, water, communication, transportation, fuel, waste disposal, etc.), economic collapse, war, electromagnetic pulse (EMP), solar flares, death of a loved one, and drought, to name a few. What you prepare for has a direct impact on how you prepare. Regardless of what you prepare for you will still need to follow the requirements of The Survival Triangle©.

Prepping allows you or your family to be ready at a moment's notice should a SLAE or SHTF situation take place. The degree of the effectiveness of your prepping will be dictated by what you prepare for. You can't be prepared for all that life with throw your way, so prepare the best you can and within your means. In the following two examples ask yourself if you would be prepared to safely endure the following events. If not, pay close attention to this handbook.

First, consider the millions who went without power amid record heat waves in June and July of 2012. The record high temperatures scorched areas from New York to Georgia, which caused severe storms. Individuals and families were without electricity and air-conditioning for over a week in extreme heat. I learned that preppers in these areas had peace of mind knowing that they were prepared to weather the event, even though their circumstances were difficult. In other words, these preppers didn't wait for a SHTF or SLAE to occur; they proactively prepared. They had plans to shelter-in-place or bug out (should it be warranted), but regardless of the action taken, they remained self-reliant. Those not prepared were scared, stressed, desperate, and in personal danger.

And finally, let's examine super storm Sandy, which devastated the East Coast on October 29, 2012. Sandy caused floods, fires, and darkness, which were all warned of well in advance of the arrival of the hurricane. Over seven million people lost power in addition to those who perished. I cannot underscore enough the importance of preparing for unknown circumstances and having access to reliable data or information from which a life-saving decision can be made.

Individuals in the above scenarios should have prepared by storing food, water, emergency supplies, fuel, medications, first aid supplies, and communication gear, to name a few.

Based on the situation, preppers are ready to bug in or bug out to a secondary shelter (a.k.a. bug-out location) using a bug-out vehicle. Having these tools and resources in place provides peace of mind knowing that you have taken care of the safety of not only yourself but that of your family or organization.

Prepping vs. Self-Reliance

It's critical to understand the difference between prepping and self-reliance. Prepping, as previously defined, ensures minimal reliance on other persons (or continuing without substantial assistance from outside resources). The key words are *minimal reliance*. Understand that there is *still* reliance. To better understand this concept, let's compare and contrast food and food storage from both prepping and self-reliance perspectives. This example can be applied to all aspects of The Survival Triangle©, although the details of each requirement will be different.

Whether you are self-reliant or a prepper, food and its storage is a critical component of survival. Food storage is just that: the storage of food for use on a daily basis during a SLAE or SHTF scenario. Let's examine this point closer. Many preppers I have had discussions with store food to consume for a specific time frame, say, six to twelve months, but give little thought to what happens when it runs out. Let's assume I have six months of stored food in my shelter and that a SLAE takes place that lasts for twelve months. Though I have six months of food, I need to be immediately concerned that I do not have enough food for the entire twelve months. It can become even more of a concern if I don't know how to hunt, garden or identify wild edibles. From a prepping perspective, I argue that preppers in all locations must be aware that the purpose of stored food, in this example, is to act as a buffer until self-reliance techniques and solutions can be implemented. The key is self-reliance, whereby you adapt to both the short- and long-term requirements of life. With a self-reliance mindset, you're focused on long-term solutions while living for today. With a self-reliance mindset, you're not waiting for a SLAE or SHTF to occur before you react; you're learning and preparing today for tomorrow. Self-reliance is in fact relying solely on one's self, family or group to provide any and all means of sustenance.

Continuing our example, self-reliance provides sustaining food sources such as vegetables, fruits, eggs, milk, meat, and grains. Self-reliance takes food and food storage one significant step forward by providing independence from modern day conveniences. In other words, you don't rely on grocery stores, internet shopping, or other means in order to live.

Self-reliance requires that you have the skills and experience to understand how to garden, understand how pH affects the growth of plants, and are aware of what fruits and vegetables can and cannot be grown next to one another. It requires that you know hunting techniques and how to harvest wild game such as deer, birds of various types, elk, squirrel, and even bear. In addition it includes animal husbandry which requires that you know how to raise, breed, and harvest cows, turkeys, llamas, chickens, ducks, rabbits, geese, horses, dairy goats, ducks, and hogs. It requires you have a complete understanding of your environment. Self-reliance allows you to harvest wild edibles, trap, fish, predict weather conditions, understand where to grow a garden, and know how to live with and within the resources of the earth. It means that you have an understanding of the interdependency between humans and the earth and use it to your advantage. For example, you must understand that rabbits are a great meat source. Three other advantages include their ability to reproduce quickly, the use of their excrement for fertilizer, and the use of their hide for different types of clothing. Self-reliance is a lifestyle for which all preppers should strive.

Most preppers will find self-reliance very challenging and, as such, homesteading may be an option. Homesteading is a subset of self-reliance whereby you minimally rely on community but by definition still relies on community resources. Homesteading is a philosophy with the goal of creating self-sufficiency. According to Hunt,

"It's about using less energy, eating wholesome local food, involving your family in the life of the community, and making wiser choices that will improve the quality of life for your family, your community, and the environment around you…" (Hunt, 2008).

To wrap up, self-reliance is a lifestyle that should be the goal of all preppers. However, not all preppers have the skills or even desire to practice self-reliance techniques. The advantage of being a prepper is that you're halfway there. Preppers often practice advanced survival techniques that support self-reliance. As a prepper you have to define what self-reliance techniques are important to you and then try them. For my family, we employ several self-reliance techniques, including gardening, food preservation (canning, water bath, dehydrating, and the use of Mylar bags), the use of herbs for healing purposes, hunting, fishing, and trapping. Will we ever be self-reliant? I'm not sure, but we're going to give it a shot.

The Ten Commandments of Prepping

The Five Tenants of Prepping

The Survival Triangle

Ten Commandments of Prepping

Many preppers have a moral compass or set of guidelines that they have established for their life. These guidelines are often dictated by religious belief, life experience, current events, and mindset. External influences may include personal goals, current events (solar flares, economy, etc.), finances, location or residency, knowledge, and skills. As a prepper it's important you understand your Ten Commandments. To establish your Ten Commandments, take into consideration your goals, beliefs, financial means, capabilities (both physical and mental), access to a network of others who believe as you do, and your commitment. The Ten Commandments can only be defined by you. The following are my Ten Commandments of Prepping:

1. God
   a) The most fundamental survival tool for any prepper is the belief in God. If you disagree with this statement, please skip this paragraph and start with number two below.
   b) God provides the foundation that gives us love, hope, joy, peace, and the desire to continue on even when those around us lose hope and faith. We can read God's word in the Bible. For me, the Bible

explains the importance of love and faith. Without something to believe in, the desire to survive or live each day becomes difficult and even painful. God teaches that life is a gift from above and every day should be enjoyed and lived to its fullest, even in the darkest of times.

2. Family

The most important relationship is that of your family and extended family. My wife and I experienced a SLAE when I had to leave the family for one year to secure work in another state. My wife was left behind to run a business and take care of the family. Needless to say, the business required her attention 24-7, and that didn't even consider the children. It was further complicated due to the fact that I was unable to return home on weekends. I was alone without my wife and family. It was extremely stressful, both in terms of our relationship and support of one another. Everyone kept telling us it would be okay and that time would make it better. It was okay, and time did make it better, but in the "eye" of the storm there was no peace. She found her coping mechanisms and I found mine, but we didn't rely on one another for support and comfort. This was our wake-up call that we would never be apart again and that family is truly all you have. In your best or worst moments, family will always love, care, and support you. They are one of the few resources you can count on.

Many families have struggles, but there will be no greater struggle than a SLAE or SHTF event. These experiences will test every fabric and the strength of your family bonds. It will require that even in the most stressful of situations you act as one unit, together, in harmony. Can you count on your family?

3. Physical well-being
    Physical well-being should be a high priority for any prepper. As such it will be presented later in this book as the Second Tenet of prepping.

4. Mental well-being
    Being mentally prepared is such a critical requirement that I also consider it in the Second Tenet of prepping. Mental well-being provides the energy and endurance to continue on when life's obstacles block your path.

Mental well-being means you remain grounded in your faith.

5. Balanced prepping

   The Survival Triangle© models the approach to balanced prepping. Balanced prepping requires that food, water, fire, and shelter be given the same priority as self-preservation. For example, when individuals think of self-preservation they often think of weapons, specifically shotguns, handguns, rifles, crossbows, etc. Yes, you need these types of tools for hunting and protection, but they're only one element of survival. Survival also requires that you have food and water to provide the energy your body needs. It requires you to have fire and somewhere to sleep at night. The opposite is also true. If you store only food and water, you are vulnerable due to a lack of protection. Each prepper has to determine their balanced approach to prepping. What's right for me may or may not be right for you.

6. Relationships

   Just as most families have a solid relationship; it's just as important to establish relationships with your neighbors and those who have a unique skill set. These unique skill sets should complement your area of expertise and those of others you may rely on. First and foremost, you must be able to count on the individuals within your family and prepping group without reservation. In a SLAE or SHTF, your neighbors will (should) be your first line of support. Together you will form a community and rely on one another. Dependent on the relationship, you may even share or barter food and services. If you lack a relationship with others, including your neighbors, you will become weary and find yourself physically guarding against those who could help you.

7. Skills

Skills include those experiences you currently have and the skills you need. Almost any skill or experience will be needed at some time in a SLAE or SHTF. It's important to recognize that your skills will be called upon, or bartered for, at any time. It's just as important to recognize the need to learn—or, at a minimum, attempt to learn—about anything that needs to be repaired, replaced, built, fabricated or designed. Once a skill has been understood and practiced, it's amazing how transferable it is to other problems or concerns. For example, once you've learned how to use a chainsaw to cut down a tree, did you know that you can use that same chainsaw to make planks of wood? Though the process and materials differ, the use of the chainsaw is the same.

8. Experience

Many times in my life I have had to rely on others to solve my problems. Late at night I had to call the plumber to fix a leak in my water line. I had to drive my truck to the mechanic to replace my brakes. The only thing I learned from this behavior was how dependent I was on others. After 9/11 this all changed. I was hungry for the experience of learning new skills. Was I scared? Yes! As I learned new skills, my confidence continued to increase. I found myself taking on larger and larger tasks. As of this writing, I'm taking courses on how to trap. I've learned how to make different types of stoves out of everyday materials. I'm learning new navigation techniques. Learning is my objective, and it should be yours, too. Not only is it fun, it could be lifesaving. Learning provides new experiences.

9. Off-Grid

As you grow in prepping experience and knowledge, it's absolutely critical that you practice, as a family or organization, living off-grid. To better understand what it may be like to live off-grid, start with the exercises in the box below.

> Off-Grid Exercises
> Remember, start off slow and easy. The goal of the first exercise is to expose your family or

organization to the difficulty of living off-grid. In addition you will quickly learn whether your preparations, skills, and experience would weather the test of time.

For your first experience, create a scenario where the power to your house will be off for four hours. When my family and I did this experiment, I quickly realized how mentally unprepared my family was. As soon as my childrens' smart phones went dead, I was in trouble. They immediately asked if I could get the generator out to charge their phones. They didn't want the generator because they were hungry or we needed light—they wanted their smart phones charged.

For your second experience, create a scenario where you lose power for a weekend. Chose a weekend during which you will live solely on your preparations. Establish ground rules for the family. For example, one condition may be that water from/for the faucet, toilet or shower is still available, but there is no hot water. Another condition is that since the stove is natural gas (i.e., not electric) it can be used. As long as the car has gas, it can be used; but once on empty, you can't go to the gas station. Create simple rules at first, and, over time, make them more complex.

> As you practice these scenarios, you and your family will quickly learn just how tough it is to survive when there is no infrastructure. In addition you will have gained experience using your prepping tools. You will also have learned that maybe you need a propane stove instead of a white gas stove. Or perhaps you didn't store enough kerosene for your heater. Though difficult, this will have been a great exercise.

10. Using resources effectively

Every prepper must learn how to be resourceful, clever, and efficient when faced with limited resources. I'm not referring to food or water, which should have already been addressed. If you don't have food or water, you have bigger things to worry about. The point to this commandment is that you need to be able to identify and use resources in ways they were not meant to be used.

Let's assume that there's been a solar flare or electromagnetic pulse that, in turn, has caused the power grid to go down. With the resources you currently have, could you live six months? If you need but don't have rope, could you make rope out of plastic grocery bags? Could you turn a one-gallon paint bucket and four soup cans into a rocket stove? From the fruits and vegetables in your garden, would you know how to properly save the seeds for use next year? Using sand, charcoal, cheese cloth, and two five-gallon buckets, would you know how to make a water filter and purification system? I think you get the point.

The Five Tenets of Prepping

The prepping community recognizes five tenets that provide the foundation of how to properly prepare and navigate the written and unwritten language of the prepper. The First Tenet of prepping is The Survival Triangle©. Because of the importance of this concept an entire chapter will be devoted to The Survival Triangle© later in the handbook.

First Tenet: The Survival Triangle©

The Survival Triangle© - Courtesy of Zion Prepper a.k.a. Bryan Foster

The Survival Triangle© models the requirements, balance, and interdependence needed for proper prepping and survival. Furthermore, each of those elements is supported by experience. The required elements are:

❖ Fire (Heat)/Shelter
❖ Water/Food
❖ Self-Preservation

Second Tenet: Physical and Mental Well-Being

The purpose of the Second Tenet is to help you understand the philosophy and importance of physical and mental well-being (but not to describe specific steps or actions). Physical and mental well-being is a personal and unique requirement that must be defined by the individual. Both physical and mental well-being requires insight, motivation, desire, and action.

In any SLAE or SHTF, the potential exists to be faced with a high level of physical and mental demand. For example, if you had to, could you walk ten, twenty, or even fifty miles without having a heart attack? Could you carry two five-gallon containers of water for a mile? In a moment's notice, could you make a life-changing decision? Are you mentally ready to live in conditions that are substandard to today's lifestyle?

Physical Well-Being

According to the Wellbeing department at Washington State University, "Physical wellbeing [sic] relates to the ability to understand what can make our body most efficient and effective, as well as the ability to recognize and respect our own limitations..." (Washington State University 2012). Physical well-being includes but is not limited to: fitness, diet, dental and eye health, immunizations, body weight, avoiding alcohol/drug abuse, and getting the right amount of sleep. Your physical well-being can be impacted by things such as gender, genetics, personal health practices, physical environment, and even income and social status. It's our job as preppers to live within our limitations and to maximize our physical well-being. As a prepper you may need to be ready to do more manual work and mental thinking than you did when times were good.

From a medical perspective, you may have to care for yourself and loved ones in ways not experienced in your lifetime. My wife and I run at least five days a week. There are many out there who would say they don't have the time. We're in the same situation. We have family commitments. We have school events. We work full-time. We have the same time constraints as most individuals, but we need fitness to be a priority. It's only one hour a day, five days a week. That's only one hour a day to maintain my weight, keep up my health, and spend quality time with my wife. No excuses on this one.

*Don't worry about how physically fit your neighbors are or aren't. Be in the best possible shape **you** can be in.*

Mental Well-Being

Just as important as your physical condition is your mental well-being. Mental well-being greatly affects physical health. Stress, depression, and anxiety can contribute to physical ailments, including digestive disorders, sleep disturbances, and lack of energy. Traumatic situations arise in everyday life, but in a SLAE or SHTF, those traumatic situations will be amplified with life and death consequences. You must be mentally ready for both natural and man-made events. You will be required to handle the decisions that must be made in a level-headed manner. As you self-reflect, you must determine if you are ready to provide the emotional support that others will need in a time of crisis. It does no good to prepare for a SLAE or SHTF scenario if you're not willing to act or make a decision when required. Are you ready to care for an older family member who has Alzheimer's disease? Are you mentally prepared to deal with the death of a loved one? Further, are you and your family mentally ready to clean and harvest wildlife for food? Sounds simple, right? But if your family is like my family, they give a name to every deer they see: Bambi. And guess what? My children don't eat Bambi. My challenge is to guide them so that they are mentally ready; it takes time.

Mental well-being plays an integral role into how you shelter-in-place and defend your shelter, water, and food, from both a physical and mental perspective. It mandates that you know how your body will react in a stressful and unpredictable environment. For example, many Iraq and Afghanistan war veterans are seeking treatment for Post Traumatic Stress Disorder (PTSD). The veterans have been taught to understand the signs of PTSD and when to seek help. Though this may be an extreme example, it demonstrates the need to understand the symptoms of stress as well as how to properly minimize the impact. Sheltering-in-place for extended periods of time, even several days, will create stress. The next time you find yourself in a stressful situation, take an inventory of your physical and mental reactions. Do you shake? Does your heart rate increase? Having this understanding allows you to minimize these stressors and deal with the possibility of having to shelter-in-place for an extended period.

Mental energy gives us the drive to endure a SHTF or SLAE while we shelter-in-place. Mental energy gives you confidence when you're feeling scared. It allows you to endure the unknown without going crazy. It allows you to provide counsel or comfort to others whom are sheltering-in-place with you. And now, how about the tough question: Are you willing to defend your family or others in your survival group to the death? There is no greater question to ask than, "Could I take a person's life?" But what if your children are starving and a gang comes to take the last of your food? What do you do? Do you watch or defend? This should be your motivation to mentally prepare before a SLAE or SHTF scenario. These are tough, tough questions, but to ignore them and wait until it happens will not help you, your family or your group. At a minimum a conversation is warranted, but even I am not sure of how to approach this topic.

Third Tenet: Redundancy

The Third Tenet of prepping is redundancy. Redundancy ensures you have alternative or multiple capabilities for each corner of The Survival Triangle©. Let's take heat for an example. If you lose electricity in the middle of the winter in Wisconsin, how will you stay warm? You might say to yourself, "I have a natural gas heater. I'll be fine." But how will you power the furnace blower without electricity? One alternative could be to have a wood-burning stove with an abundant supply of wood. A second option would be to use a propane heater such as a torpedo heater or a Big Buddy. A third option would be to purchase a kerosene heater with extra wicks and enough kerosene to carry you for two or three weeks. The point is that if one source fails, you should have multiple backup technologies, albeit some simple, to solve the problem. Jack Spirko of The Survival Podcast© has a mantra that goes, "Two is one, one is none, and three is for me." It means, for example, that if you have two heaters, you really only have one, in that if one fails, you have one left. If you only have one heater and it fails, then you are left with none. The best advice is to have three heaters, and should one fail, you have two backup units. Another important point of this concept is to ensure that your redundant units are interchangeable. Continuing the example above, if one heater fails, and assuming the units are similar models, you could use the parts from one to repair the other. You now have the advantage of not only redundancy but also interchangeability amongst parts.

Fourth Tenet: Forming a Community

The Fourth Tenet of prepping is to take care of yourself and your family or group through community. This is the reason you prepare in the first place. This tenet was my most challenging. Before establishing a reliable community of preppers I had to convince my wife that prepping had a purpose. Initially my wife was reluctant to support me in my prepping efforts. I knew that to prepare effectively, I needed to gain the support of my spouse and family. Prepping is a life-changing philosophy that many people have never heard of or considered. She knew little to nothing about what I was doing—and, frankly, neither did I. In her own words, she thought I was nuts.

At first she saw my purchases as wasteful and not practical. When I received stoves, MREs, and other types of survival supplies in the mail, she could not fathom ever having to use the equipment. I had to slowly ease her into the idea and not come on strong or discuss doomsday scenarios. At first the idea was overwhelming for her. She didn't understand why we had to prepare for something that might not happen. She was content doing the weekly shopping, which simply carried us through until her next trip to the grocery store. However, as she became more cognizant of natural disasters across the country, she was able to relate to what I was doing. She saw how important it was to have water, food, heat, and protection. In essence, she had to define prepping for herself. Now she's actively involved in prepping, and she makes recommendations on what and when to buy items for our preps. Prepping gives my wife peace of mind as a mother and wife. She is a prepper in her own right as well as the wife of a prepper.

As a family, we started out slowly due to limited resources, but now even our children understand the concept of prepping. We explain why we prep and they watch how we prep. They actively engage us in questions. Frankly, they love the fact that they can go to our preps and "shop" for any of the five brands of cereal we have.

The following questions may be useful as you discuss prepping with your spouse, partner, family or friends and attempt to gain their support:

- Do you feel it's important to be prepared for manmade or natural events?
- Do you feel it's worth the time and investment to be prepared for something we can't predict?
- What are some of the steps we should take together to prepare? (start small with this one).
- What do you know about prepping other than what you see on television (Doomsday Preppers)?
- How and what do we teach our children about prepping?
- What kinds of events do you think we should be prepared for (e.g., earthquake, economic collapse, etc.)?
- Should we involve family or other members in our prepping activities?

Once my wife understood and supported my prepping endeavors I began to form a community of like-minded individuals. Having a community outside of your family is important. In a true SHTF situation, you can only shelter-in-place so long before outsiders find you and your supplies. Thus you need to partner with your neighbors, friends or other individuals who prepare as you do. In these groups you learn a new way of life. It could possibly be a life based not on money (if there has been an economic collapse), but on the barter and group system, in which you trade expertise (e.g., construction, plumbing, chemistry, forestry, etc.) or goods (e.g., silver, hardware, food, water, etc.) for what you need. These small groups will provide protection to all individuals, but will expect you to do the same. Individuals will be accepted into these groups as they demonstrate the value they bring through their skills and use of those skills. The premise behind this tenet is that you need to reach out to others before others reach out to you. If you don't reach out prior to a SLAE or SHTF, you could compromise the security of you or your family. You will read this theme several times throughout this book and series. You need to be integrated and connected with other preppers or individuals who want to partner and support each other during a SLAE or SHTF scenario.

Because community is critical to survival, I have developed a relationship with a community of other preppers. Our group consists of fewer than twenty people, but we form a tight-knit community. Within the community are multiple disciplines and experiences, including mechanical and electrical engineering, architecture, law enforcement, iron- and woodworking, construction, and cooking. Most of the community members are retired, hence the experience, and supportive of one another. Regardless of how tight knit a group is, always remember that the individuals within that group or community are still individuals. Though they support the group, they will always take care of themselves first; especially when times get tough. That is simply human nature.

As a beginning prepper, I had a hard time finding other preppers I wanted to learn from and with whom I wanted to share. The reason is that my perception was that others would see me as a whacko or, worse, deranged. I was also concerned if others knew my belief it would jeopardize my professional career. For those preppers who feel as I do, it makes it even more difficult, as it's a double-edged sword. As I tried to keep my anonymity, I had to divulge enough information to continue to grow within the prepper community and expand my network. I eventually put everything in perspective and realized that everyone prepares for something. What I prepare for is no different than when my wife prepares dinner. She buys the food one week in advance and in the right amounts. When she needs it, it's there ready to be used. In simplistic terms, this was what I was doing.

In my experience I've learned that you must first be accepted by an individual or individuals within the prepper community to become part of the community. To form your community or become a part of one, there are many great tools, such as YouTube, Facebook, Twitter, blogTV, blogs, and websites. I used these tools to introduce myself to the prepper community. I started by making short five- to six-minute videos and posting them to YouTube. Other preppers commented or e-mailed me with ideas. A well-known prepper on YouTube reached out to me and hence my network was created. He gave me a "shout out," which is basically a recommendation for others to visit my YouTube channel. Before I knew it, I was associated with a great community.

There are also local forums on the Internet specific to each county in each state; these are a good place to start. There are podcasts such as The Survival Podcast with Jack Spirko and American Preppers Network that provide excellent information. Remember that the online prepping community doesn't necessarily have an open door, but, at the same time, it's not closed. You simply have to reach out and the community will reach back.

Having and being part of a community is the foundation of prepping

<u>Fifth Tenet: Silence</u>

The Fifth Tenet of prepping is silence. At first it may seem to be in direct conflict with the Fourth Tenet of prepping, but upon further understanding, you will see that it is not. The Fifth Tenet simply means that you must be extremely selective in deciding whom to talk to about your prepping. The more you divulge about yourself and your preparations, the more you expose yourself. In a SHTF situation, individuals will remember your discussions, recall your provisions, and perhaps rely on you for support. In other words, the possibility exists that others may turn to you for food/water, heat/shelter, and protection. Before you know it, you'll be feeding, protecting, and sheltering non-preppers en masse, who will come to expect it. Once you stop feeding, protecting, and sheltering these individuals, they may become desperate and even violent.

In addition there is the potential that individuals, and yes, even gangs, may become aware of your support to others. This will identify you as a "target," and the potential exists that you may have to defend your stores.

You must also be careful in what you wear as it can inadvertently "advertise" or be interpreted that you're a person who can help or has survival knowledge or skills. What I mean by advertising is visually alerting others that somehow you're "different." For example, wearing a paracord bracelet visually shows others that you may be associated with a prepper or survival community as these bracelets are not common outside of the communities. Wearing camouflage constantly is a sign that you may have outdoor skills, even if you don't. The point is that how and what you communicate (yes, even how you dress) may provide needless signals to others. In all cases, the less information to others, the better.

You may volunteer or be called upon to take care of others if and when possible, but you want to position yourself in such a manner that others don't come to you but you go to them. I argue that preppers should share knowledge and train others. This allows for the greater good of all as more people become self-sufficient.

It's incumbent upon preppers to teach others the basic principles of prepping and survival. Future books in *The Prepper's Survival Guide Series* will discuss how to reach out to other preppers, establish relationships, grow networks, and better understand prepping and survival skills. Future books will also include the prepping sources (e.g., websites, podcasts, blogs, etc.) I used to better myself and improve my prepping skills, network, and communication. Prepping is a delicate balance of self-preservation, helping others where possible, expanding your network, and maintaining privacy.

The Survival Triangle©

You can consider yourself a prepper when you are PREPARED, PREPARED, AND PREPARED. If you try and prepare after a SLAE it's too late. You will have to survive with what you have available. By the time you realize you don't have or are low on critical supplies, I can guarantee you that the staples such as milk, bread, sugar, flour, and bottled water will be gone. This is why you prepare in advance with a focus on understanding The Survival Triangle©. Yet again, it's important to understand that The Survival Triangle© models the requirements, balance, and interdependence needed to be properly prepared for numerous SHTF scenarios. Furthermore, each of those elements is supported by experience.

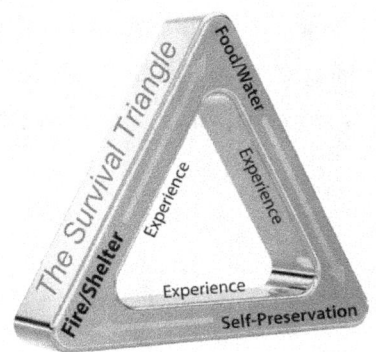

The Survival Triangle© - Courtesy of Zion Prepper a.k.a. Bryan Foster

On each corner of The Survival Triangle© is a requirement that must be satisfied in order to be safely and properly prepared. They are:

- ❖ Fire (Heat)/Shelter
- ❖ Water/Food
- ❖ Self-Preservation

Should any one element or corner be missing, your survival or that of your family or group is in jeopardy. For example, without the food or water elements, it may not matter if you have shelter, heat or skills in self-preservation. The reason is simple; you will be challenged to remain hydrated and have the protein you need to maintain proper nutrition. Without self-preservation skills you may not be able to mentally function in a SLAE or know how to properly handle a weapon. Let's now discuss each element of The Survival Triangle© to better understand their interdependence, including a detailed description of what to prepare.

Bryan and Camden Foster

Water

Water

You need water for many reasons, such as to stay hydrated, cook, bathe, brush your teeth, care for animals, and grow plants. In the human body, water helps regulate body temperature (through sweat), protects the nervous system, keeps the skin moist, rids the body of waste, and cushions the joints — a critical component of survival. Remember, the average human body is composed of sixty-five percent water. As such, the typical rule of thumb is that a human can survive three minutes without air, three hours without shelter (i.e., a subzero winter), *three days without water*, and three weeks without food. Before you ever need to shelter-in-place, remember the rule of 2 + 2 that helps with planning. The rule states when you shelter-in-place you need 2 quarts of water for drinking per day + 2 quarts of water for cooking and hygiene per person per day. However, I highly recommend you store one gallon of water per day per person for drinking and two quarts of water per person per day for cooking and hygiene.

After 24 hours without water, dehydration can set in. According to the National Institutes of Health symptoms of dehydration include dry or sticky mouth, an inability to produce tears, little to no urine output, lethargy, and sunken eyes. Without water, the ability to breathe becomes much more difficult. Lung function uses up to one pint of water every day, decreasing the body's moisture level through exhalation.

Many SHTF or SLAE scenarios won't cause a panic because running water will be available and most events will not last beyond several days. But what if you had to shelter-in-place and running water was not available? Let's say you plan to store a one-month supply of water for a family of five. In this case, you would need 150 gallons of water (thirty days multiplied by five family members equals 150 gallons). How would you store 150 gallons of water and where would you store it?

How much water you can store will depend on five things:

- the number of members in your family, group, or organization,
- the amount of storage you have,
- how you organize your storage area,
- how you store your water, and
- what your mobility is (for example, will you be moving water from your shelter to your vehicle as you move locations?)

Remember, water is heavy. It weighs about 8.35 pounds per gallon. If you shelter-in-place, your storage conditions will be different than if you're in your bug-out vehicle (BOV) headed to your bug-out location (BOL). In other words, storing water in a house is different than storing water in a moving vehicle.

It's important to understand how water is classified and also understand the fact that ninety-seven percent of the water on earth is salt water. So if ninety-seven percent of the water on earth is salt water, how do you find clean drinking (also known as potable) water? First let's distinguish between potable and non-potable water sources:

- Potable water is water of a sufficiently high enough quality that it can be consumed with a low risk of immediate or long-term harm.
- Non-potable water is water that is not of drinkable quality and therefore is not for consumption.

Because water is a renewable resource there are many sources to consider, from the simple to the complex. Some will be on high ground, while others will be on lower ground. Some will be potable, while others are non-potable. Some will provide large quantities of water whereas others provide very little water. Some will provide water in a different form, such as snow, while others will offer water that is difficult to capture, such as condensation. Whatever the source, it's water — and once filtered and purified it will save your life.

Listed below are sources of water as well as storage options:

- Bottled water by the gallon or pint.
- Portable water bladders such as the WaterBob™ or Aqua Pod™.
  - Portable water bladders are made of high density polyethylene. They are portable and can contain up to 100 gallons of water.
  - They have the advantage of being easily stored until needed, can hold large volumes of water, are cost-effective at around twenty-five dollars (at the time of this writing), and remain in a bathtub, therefore minimizing the amount of space required. The disadvantage is that you have to fill the bladder before a SHTF event or before water becomes unavailable
- Outside rain barrels to capture runoff water (this assumes you have rain).
- Two-liter soda bottles. A cheap and effective way to store emergency water.

You can store water in milk jugs, but do not use it for

drinking. This water should only be used for things like bathing, washing clothes, or other similar tasks.

- Five-gallon stackable water containers. A great option, but slightly pricier.
- Water pouches such as those by Datrex™.
- Washer.
  - Many people don't consider this option, but a washer is meant to hold and retain gallons of water without leaking. This makes it a great water storage vessel.

If times get desperate you can find water in the following locations:

- Water heater

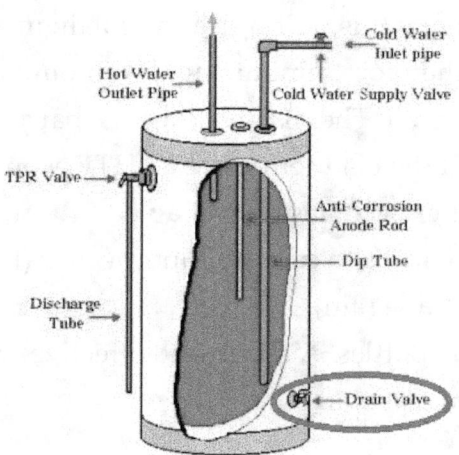

In an emergency open the drain valve of your water heater for water

- Water pipes throughout the house
- Water can also be found in canned foods, including soups, vegetables, and fruits. When you eat canned foods never discard the water; either drink it immediately or store it for later use.
- Fire hydrants
- If you live in a cold climate, you may have access to snow. However, snow as a source of water is only a good choice if it's from a relatively clean source of water.

Don't eat snow or ice directly as it will lower your body temperature and potentially lead to dehydration. Instead, heat the snow or ice to melt it.

- Surface water, such as lakes and rivers, provides an excellent source.
- Neighbors
- Wells are another great source of water; however, you must remember to have a manual pump in the event that electricity is not available.
- Cisterns which are watertight structures used to store water. Most often the water found in a cistern comes from rain.

Last resort options include:
- Toilet water stored in the cistern.
  - Even though a toilet will provide about one to six gallons of water, including what's in the tank or cistern, it contains microorganisms as well as cleaning chemicals. Toilet water must be brought to a rolling boil or treated with chemicals before use.
- Water beds
  - Waterbeds contain a significant amount of stagnant water and is a haven for microorganisms.
- Swimming pools and/or hot tubs
- Fish tank

Once again, these are last resort options that require proper purification before use. This list should begin to get you thinking about what options are available to you.

Remember to store water in a cool, dark area and replace every six to twelve months. If water storage containers/bottles are not marked with an expiration date, label each one with the current date and replace the water at least once per year.

Liquids *Not* to Consume

In any situation where water is scarce, there are several liquids that should <u>**not**</u> be consumed at any time. First, and contrary to popular belief, **do not** drink urine. Urine is excreted from your body for a reason. It is ninety-five percent water, but the remaining five percent is **waste** that includes urea, dissolved salts and organic compounds. Don't drink it. Second, never drink alcohol. Alcohol is a diuretic, which is the reason you urinate so much while drinking. Because of the frequent urination and lack of water you become dehydrated and get that classic hangover headache. Third, don't drink coffee. It's another diuretic that causes you to urinate frequently and can lead to dehydration. Other natural diuretics include apple cider vinegar, green tea, cranberry juice, asparagus, oats, lettuce, and cabbage; however, eaten in small quantities these should cause no concern about dehydration.

Filtration and Purification

As previously indicated, your water may require filtration prior to consumption. Depending on the source of your water, it may contain particles such as wood, leaves, mud, and rocks that need to be filtered out. The simplest and most effective means of filtering water is to use cheesecloth or coffee filters. In a survival situation, use your clothes. The goal is to remove as many of the big particles as possible. If the water is muddy or cloudy, let it sit for up to twelve hours; then slowly ladle or remove the water without disturbing any material that may have settled to the bottom of the container.

Next you must purify your water. In order to understand the importance of purifying water, it's helpful to know why it needs to be purified. Water contains pathogens, or infectious agents. Two common pathogens found in water are cryptosporidium (sometimes called crypto) and giardia.

Cryptosporidiosis is a parasitic disease that affects the intestines. Cryptosporidium causes diarrhea, which can lead to dehydration if not carefully watched. Symptoms of cryptosporidiosis typically occur two to ten days after ingestion and last for a few weeks. Cryptosporidium can only be killed by bringing water to a rolling boil. It is highly resistant to chlorine treatment; therefore, chemical disinfectants have been shown not to be 100 percent effective in killing it.

Giardia is another parasite that affects the small intestines. Symptoms often appear one to two weeks after ingestion and include, but are not limited to, diarrhea (watch out for dehydration), stomach cramps, nausea, and an upset stomach. These symptoms can last anywhere from one to two weeks. The Centers for Disease Control and Prevention states that "to kill or inactivate giardia, bring your water to a rolling boil for one minute (at elevations above 6,500 feet, boil for three minutes). Water should then be allowed to cool, stored in a clean sanitized container with a tight cover, and refrigerated..." (*Prevention*, 2006).

Bringing water to a rolling boil per the CDC guidelines is the best way to eradicate both cryptosporidium and giardia and to insure the safety of your drinking water. In addition, this method of purification is highly cost-effective (starting a fire in nature to boil water is essentially free). Other water diseases and/or pathogens include but are not limited to the following:

- Dysentery
- Typhoid
- E. coli
- Salmonella
- Hepatitis
- Rotavirus
- Norovirus (formerly Norwalk)

If you have doubts about the quality of the water, boil it for a minimum of two minutes or chemically treat it. Examples of chemical treatment include:

- Calcium hypochlorite

  Also called pool shock or HTH (high-test hypochlorite), this chemical is often used in swimming pools. Make sure you purchase "pure" calcium hypochlorite (sixty-five to seventy percent grade) that contains no other chemicals (e.g., clarifiers, anti-fungals, etc.). Follow the guidelines from the U.S. Army Center for Health Promotion and Preventive Medicine to make a diluted solution of calcium hypochlorite. You will add this solution to your main water supply to disinfect it. Do not drink the solution itself.

  o Place one heaping tablespoon of calcium hypochlorite in two gallons of water and wait for it to dissolve. Label this container "Calcium Hypochlorite Concentrate. DO NOT DRINK" and include the date you made it.

  o Once it's dissolved, add the concentrated solution you just made to your main supply of water to disinfect it. The suggested ratio is one part chlorine solution to 100 parts water. This is equivalent to one pint of solution for every twelve and a half gallons of water (eight pints equals one gallon).

o Store any remaining calcium hypochlorite material (i.e., what's left in the package) in a cool, dry place and label appropriately.

- Chlorine bleach

This is a cheap and effective means of purifying water. Do not use scented bleaches, color-safe bleaches or bleaches with added cleaners. Water treated with bleach, on average, will keep for approximately six to twelve months.

o The Washington State Department of Health (Health, 2009) has created the following guidelines:

See the following page for guidelines.

Treating Water with a 5-6 Percent Liquid Chlorine Bleach Solution

Volume of Water to be Treated	Treating Clear/Cloudy Water: Bleach Solution to Add	Treating Cloudy, Very Cold, or Surface Water: Bleach Solution to Add
1 quart/1 liter	3 drops	5 drops
1/2 gallon/2 quarts/2 liters	5 drops	10 drops
1 gallon	1/8 teaspoon (approximately 10 drops)	1/4 teaspoon
5 gallons	1/2 teaspoon	1 teaspoon
10 gallons	1 teaspoon	2 teaspoons

o Wait one hour before drinking water treated with chlorine bleach. If there is a bleach taste or odor, pour the water to be used back and forth between two pitchers or pans a couple of times. This will diminish the bleach odor.

__Warning: Bleach can be extremely poisonous to the human body if not used properly and in the right amounts.__

- Potassium permanganate

This is another cheap and easy way to purify water. Potassium permanganate crystals can be bought at hardware stores.

o Add three or four crystals per quart of water (or until the water stains a light pink) and let the water sit for thirty minutes.

Water treated with potassium permanganate can also be used as a disinfectant for cleaning wounds.

o Simply add crystals one by one until the water turns pink. You need a solution of approximately 0.01 percent, which requires about three or four crystals per quart of water.

- Purification tablets

These typically contain either iodine or chlorine and should be used according to the manufacturer's instructions.

- Tincture of iodine (two percent)

Iodine is very effective against bacteria, viruses, and protozoa with the exception of cryptosporidium. When using iodine you must remember that the colder the water the longer it takes to disinfect. Most importantly, iodine is to be used on a short-term basis only. Iodine can be poisonous to humans, especially to young children. In addition you should be aware that iodine has a terrible taste. This is one of my least favorite methods of water purification.

   o   If the water is mostly clear, use four drops of iodine per quart of water (sixteen drops of iodine per gallon).
   o   If the water is cloudy and you were unable to filter the water, use eight drops of iodine per quart (thirty-two drops per gallon).

Wait one hour before drinking water treated with tincture of iodine.

WARNING: Pregnant, nursing women or anyone with a thyroid condition should not use this method.

Non-chemical means of water purification include:

- Distillation. A process that can be used at home and in nature. Distillation at home utilizes a stove, large cooking pot, cooking pot lid, and a cup to capture purified water in the form of steam. In nature the earth is used to capture purified water based on temperature differences.
- Filtration units such as the Berkey™, the AquaRain™ Natural Water Filter, and the MSR Autoflow™ Gravity Water Filter.
- Hand-pump filters such as the MiniWorks EX™ Hand Pump Filter and the Katadyn™ Mini Ultralight Water Filter.
- Microfiltration water filters. These remove contaminants by passing water through a membrane. An example is the Katadyn™ Pocket filter.
- Survival straws. These use a highly efficient water purification system to destroy the harmful bacteria and viruses that exist in most sources of water.

Food

Food

Food provides the protein and nutrition necessary to produce energy within the body and sustain life. In addition, food provides nutrients that help keep our bones, hair, nails, and skin strong and flexible. In a SHTF situation, food can even be used to trade or barter for other necessities. Beyond this guide, you can further explore the importance of water and food from a prepper perspective in *The Prepper's Survival Guide: A Guide to Water and Food*.

On average, a person can go three weeks without food. Factors that will have a direct impact on how long you can go without food include the following:

- your health
- your metabolism
- your ratio of body fat to muscle
- your hydration level
- the temperature of your environment
- the work you are performing

As with every element of The Survival Triangle©, you must have food already stored before you have to shelter-in-place. There are two types of food supplies: short-term and long-term. Short-term foods supplies typically last three days to six months and are high in protein and calories, whereas the purpose of long-term food supplies is to feed you and your family beyond six months, with one year being the goal. The amount of food you store will be based on your diet, weight, health, and number of people to feed. You will have to determine the amount (pounds) and types of food that are appropriate to you, your family or group. There is no magic formula for the amount of food to store but there are food storage serving matrixes that can be used as guidelines. For example, one food storage serving matrix recommends that 400 pounds of wheat be stored per person, which provides one year of servings. When determining how much food to store you need to consider how many calories per day you need to maintain your health and strength. In general most adults need between 1,500 – 3,000 calories per day. If you're new to prepping start your food supply with the basics. Here are several ideas on where to start:

- Grains - These typically store well for ten years, but wheat can last up to twenty years if stored properly. Grains include wheat berries, quinoa, oats, barley, flaxseed, and millet.
- Dried legumes (e.g., soybeans, split peas, and lentils) - Properly stored, these can last for seven to ten years.

- Dried fruits and vegetables - These can be kept for seven to ten years if properly stored.
- Rice - Properly stored, rice can be kept for seven to ten years.
- Corn - According to the Federal Emergency Management Administration, (FEMA), dried corn can be stored indefinitely, provided that it is properly stored in appropriate containers and isn't contaminated by insects, moisture, or other environmental contaminants.
- Honey - Never spoils.
- Dry milk - This will last up to five years if stored properly.

-

Other foods to consider include the following:

- MREs (Meals-Ready-to-Eat) - An MRE is a self-contained, individual field ration in lightweight packaging that the United States military provides for its service members. MREs are designed for use in combat or other field conditions where organized food facilities are not available.
- Freeze-dried foods - These can be stored for up to twenty-five years in proper storage conditions. Examples of freeze-dried foods include a variety of fruits, vegetables, and complete meals produced by commercial companies such as Mountain House™.

- Dehydrated foods - Examples include iodized salt, white flour, cracked wheat cereal, quick oats, rolled oats, buttermilk powder, and peanut butter powder.
- Comfort foods such as candy, canned soups, cookies, spaghetti, hamburgers, hot dogs, corn on the cob, chili, and ice cream.
- Fats and Oils

When storing food, don't forget items like spices, salt, pepper, vinegar, bouillon cubes, sugar, vegetable oil, shortening, baking powder, baking soda, yeast, and dry soup mixes. These items will help to give your food more flavors and make unfamiliar foods more appealing.

<u>Food Preservation</u>

Food preservation is the process of stopping or slowing spoilage in order to allow for longer storage time frames. Over time, foods lose their nutritional value, taste, and eventually become inedible. The better they are preserved the longer they last. Preservation involves preventing the growth of microorganisms such as bacteria and fungi as well as the oxidation of fats. Examples of food preservation methods include:

<u>Canning</u>

Canning is an example of a highly efficient method of preserving food. Dr. Brian Nummer of Utah State University Cooperative Extension has published a fact sheet to help explain canning. As Dr. Nummer explains:

> "For the purpose of this fact sheet, 'canned foods' refer to foods canned in liquid. Dry pack canned goods are not included. Canned foods are safe alternatives to fresh and frozen foods and help meet dietary needs and avoid preservatives. Proper storage can greatly increase the shelf life and quality of canned foods.
>
> <u>Quality & Purchase</u>. Canned foods can either be purchased commercially or home canned. Home canned foods should be canned using research-tested recipes and processes like those found in the USDA Complete Guide to Canning or in Cooperative Extension publications. Use only the best quality foods to can at home. Home canning processes can never improve the quality of foods. Commercially canned foods are superior to home canned for food storage. Commercial canners can closely control quality and safety to produce the best product. Commercially canned foods for storage can be purchased at grocery stores and

similar outlets. Avoid budget resellers (e.g., scratch and dent sales, dollar stores, etc.). Purchase canned foods in either cans or jars. Avoid rusted, dented, scratched, or bulging cans.

Packaging. Foods are commercially canned in glass jars with lids, metal cans, or special metal-Mylar®-type pouches. All of these materials are suitable for food storage. Home canners should only can in mason-style canning jars with two piece metal lids as recommended by the *USDA Complete Guide to Canning*. Home canning in metal cans or metal-Mylar®-type pouches requires special knowledge and equipment. Improper processing of home canned foods could lead to Clostridium botulinum food poisoning.

Storage Conditions. Carefully label all home canned or commercially canned food containers. We recommend labeling purchase date (month & year) on can lid with marker. Store all canned food in cool, dark, dry space away from furnaces, pipes, and places where temperatures change like un-insulated attics. Do not allow sealed cans or glass jars to freeze. Freezing changes food textures, and leads to rust, bursting cans, and broken seals that may let in harmful bacteria. Always store metal cans off of the floor, especially bare concrete. Moisture can wick up to cans and encourage rusting.

Nutrition & Allergies. Canned foods maintain mineral content for entire shelf life. Vitamins A & C will decrease rapidly after fruits and vegetables are picked and cooked. Vitamins are lost during heating processes; however, once canned, vitamin A & C loss slows to 5- 20% per year. Other vitamins remain close to fresh food levels. Salt or sugar are not necessary for safe canning and only added for flavoring. Be sure to label canned goods with ingredients when canning mixed foods like sauces.

Shelf Life. As a general rule, unopened home canned foods have a shelf life of one year and should be used before 2 years. Commercially canned foods should retain their best quality until the expiration code date on the can. This date is usually 2-5 years from the manufacture date. High acid foods usually have a shorter shelf life than low acid foods. For emergency storage, commercially canned foods in metal or jars will remain safe to consume as long as the seal has not been broken. (That is not to say the quality will be retained for that long). Foods "canned" in metal-Mylar®-type pouches will also have a best-if-used by date on them. The longest shelf life tested of this type of packaging has been 8-10 years (personal communication U.S. Military MREs). Therefore, storage for longer than 10 years is not recommended..." (Nummer 2008).

Dehydration

Dehydration is a process of food preservation that works by removing water from the food, which inhibits the growth of microorganisms.

- Dehydrated food can be stored for as long as thirty years in proper storage conditions. Examples include iodized salt, white flour, cracked wheat cereal, quick oats, rolled oats, buttermilk powder, and peanut butter powder.

Dry-pack method

This is the current method of the Latter-Day Saints. It preserves food in #10 steel cans to prevent the growth of microorganisms, yeast, and mold. Oxygen absorbers are used to minimize the amount of air in the can and the cans are sealed using a dry-pack canning machine. The cans are labeled with the contents and date. They can be stored safely for the longest possible shelf life.

- Foodstoragemadeeasy.net provides guidelines on how much of various food types can be stored in #10 cans and five-gallon buckets.

Food Item	#10 Can	5 Gallon Bucket
Wheat	5 pounds	37 pounds
White Flour	4.5 pounds	33 pounds
Cornmeal	4.3 pounds	33 pounds
Popcorn	5 pounds	37 pounds
Rolled Oats	2.5 pounds	20 pounds
White Rice	5.3 pounds	36 pounds
Spaghetti	N/A	30 pounds
Macaroni	3.1 pounds	21 pounds
Dried Beans	5.6 pounds	35 pounds
Lima Beans	5.4 pounds	35 pounds
Soy Beans	5 pounds	33 pounds
Split Peas	5 pounds	33 pounds
Lentils	5.5 pounds	35 pounds
White Sugar	5.7 pounds	35 pounds
Brown Sugar	4.42 pounds	33 pounds
Powdered Milk	3 pounds	29 pounds
Powdered Eggs	2.6 pounds	20 pounds

Courtesy of foodstoragemadeeasy.net

Freeze-dried foods

Freeze-drying foods is essentially a dehydration process whereby food is frozen followed by reducing the surrounding pressure. By doing this the frozen water sublimates; i.e., the water goes from solid phase to gas phase. The food is then sealed to prevent water from being reabsorbed by the food. The freeze-dried process preserves food, allows it to be stored at room temperature, protects it against spoilage, does not cause shrinkage (of the food), and is easily reconstituted by adding water. Freeze-dried foods weigh less and take up less space than their fresh counterparts, so they are easier to transport. Freeze-dried food can be stored for up to twenty-five years in proper storage conditions. Examples include buffalo-style chicken, spaghetti, beef stew, all types of fruits, green beans, corn, and beef stroganoff with noodles.

Freezing

Freezing is typically easy to do and very straightforward. To freeze food or other perishables, you simply clean them, proportion according to size or volume (typically by weight), place in a protective container, and place in freezer. The advantages of freezing food are:

- Almost all foods can be frozen.
- Foods can be frozen in less time when compared to other processes such as canning or dehydration.
- Flavor, color, and nutritional value are retained.
- Proportion control.

But what about when you lose power for an extended period of time? As Dr. Sterling Silverman, a.k.a. Survival Doc, writes:

"Freezing is an easy and convenient method of food preservation. It is also very good at retaining the nutritional value of your food. There is one huge and obvious disadvantage to freezing: What happens when the electricity goes off? You can invest in a gasoline or propane-powered generator to keep your freezer running during power outages. But eventually you are going to run out of fuel for your generator. For that reason I suggest that you do not rely on your freezer for your primary method of food storage. If you are a hunter or have a garden and prefer freezing to canning, that is fine. Hopefully you will have a generator and will be able to consume your frozen foods before you run out of fuel. But you should also have a stash of foods that do not require freezing for those longer emergencies.

When the power goes out the food in a full freestanding freezer will be safe for about two days, providing you don't open the door too much. A chest-type freezer is much more desirable than an upright freezer because it will retain the cold longer. Remember that the foods at greatest risk are meat, poultry, and foods containing dairy products..." (Silverman 2012)

The National Center for Food Preservation (Harison, 2006) states that storage containers for freezer use should not become brittle or crack at low temperatures. They should be the following:

- resistant to moisture vapor
- durable and leak-proof
- resistant to oil, grease, and water
- able to protect foods from absorbing flavors or odors
- easy to seal
- easy to mark

Vacuum sealing

A vacuum sealer can be used to remove air from a bag or container. Without oxygen, microbes are unable to form. Vacuum sealing can be used in conjunction with other preservation methods. Upfront costs for this method include the vacuum sealer and plastic bags. The purchase of additional plastic bags, which can be specific to a particular brand or model of vacuum sealer, is an ongoing cost.

Food Storage Shelf Life

Food storage is absolutely critical to maintain the nutrients and life of your foods. As previously described, there are many food preservation options from which to select. Once you've determined the most effective way to store your food it's critical to understand shelf life. As Joan Crain (Crain, 2007) explains:

> "The question frequently asked is, 'What is the shelf life of my food storage?' First, let's define 'food storage' and 'shelf life.'
>
> Food storage generally refers to long-term foods that are low in moisture and can be stored for a long time.
>
> Shelf life is defined in two ways:
>
> 'best if used by' – the length of time foods are best in taste and nutrition.
>
> 'life sustaining' food shelf life – the length of time foods can be stored and still edible.
>
> There can be a big time difference between these two types of food products. Foods bought at the grocery store can have a shelf life of a few days to

several years, depending on the type of food, the storage conditions, and the packaging. That's why those products have a 'best if used by' date which is required by law.

The 'life sustaining' foods are those that are packaged specifically for long-term storage. The estimated shelf life for many of these products has increased to 30 years or more (see chart below).

If stored more than 30 years, taste and nutritional quality will decline, depending on the quality of the food when first packaged. However, studies have shown that these foods, even if stored past their designated time, retain their calories and calories will sustain life in an emergency and prevent starvation.

Food storage shelf life for long term food storage depends on four main criteria:

Temperature
Moisture
Oxygen
Light

Let's look at these one at a time.

Temperature

Foods stored at room temperature or cooler (75°F/24°C or lower) will be nutritious and edible much longer than previously thought according to findings of recent scientific studies. Foods stored at 50°F to 60°F (which is optimal) will last longer than foods stored at higher temperatures. Heat absolutely destroys food and its nutritional value. Proteins break down and some vitamins will be destroyed. Taste, color, and smell of some foods may also change.

Moisture

The reason long term food storage is dehydrated or freeze-dried is to eliminate moisture. Too much moisture promotes an atmosphere where microorganisms can grow and chemical reaction in foods causing deterioration that ultimately can sicken us.

Oxygen

Too much oxygen can deteriorate foods and promote the growth of microorganisms, especially in fats, vitamins, and food colors. That is the reason to use oxygen absorbers when dry packing your own food products.

Light

Exposure to too much light can cause deterioration of foods. In particular it affects food colors, vitamin loss, fats and oils, and proteins. Keep long-term food storage in low light areas for longest shelf life.

Long-Term Food Shelf Life Chart
(The years listed for shelf life assumes ideal storage conditions, i.e., low moisture, low light, cool temperatures, and low oxygen content.)"

See the following two pages for Long-Term Food Shelf Life Charts

Food	"Life Sustaining" Shelf-Life Estimates (In Years)
Apple slices	30
Alfalfa Seeds	8
Bakers Flour	15
Barley	10
Black Turtle Beans	15 - 20
Blackeye Peas	15 -20
Buckwheat	15
Butter/margarine Powder	15
Cocoa Powder	15
Cornmeal	5
Cracked wheat	25
Durham Wheat	8-12
Flax	8-12
Flour (white)	10-20
Flour (whole wheat)	10-20
Garbanzo Beans	15 - 20
Garden Seeds	4
Gluten	5
Granola	5
Honey, Salt and Sugar	Indefinitely
Hulled Oats	30
Kidney Beans	20
Lentils	20
Lima Beans	20
Millet	8-12
Morning Moo	10

Food	"Life Sustaining" Shelf-Life Estimates (In Years)
Onions	8-12
Pasta	30
Pearled Oats	10
Pink Beans	20 - 30
Pinto Beans	30+
Potatoes (flakes, slices, diced)	30
Powdered Eggs	15
Powdered Milk	20
Quinoa	8
Rice (brown)	6 months
Rice (white)	25+
Rolled Oats	30
Rye	8
Small Red Beans	8-10
Soy Beans	8-10
Special bakery wheat	25
Spelt	12
Sprouting Seeds	4-5
Triticale	8-12
TVP	15 - 20
Unbleached Flour	5
Vegetables (most)	20-30
Wheat (hard white)	30
Wheat (hard red)	30+
Wheat flakes	5
Whey Powder	15
Yeast	2

(Crain, 2007)

Herbs

Herbs should also be included in any prepper's food stores. Herbs provide a natural means of soothing, maintaining, and healing the human body in addition to making food more flavorful. If the world were to experience a true pandemic, herbs would be one option to replace medicine due to lack of availability. Below are descriptions of the health benefits of some common herbs. This is by no means a complete list. Furthermore, the health benefits listed below are only a sampling of the reasons why you should include herbs in your food preps.

- Basil inhibits the growth of several types of bacteria. It also has anti-inflammatory effects and is a source of vitamin A, vitamin K, calcium, manganese, and magnesium.

- Chamomile acts as a mild relaxant to combat depression, stress, and anxiety. It is also a muscle relaxant, helps the skin in cases of burns and allergies, and works as a sleep aid, cold fighter, and wound healer.

- Cilantro has anti-inflammatory properties, relieves stomach gas, and has protective properties against bacterial infection. It also helps to increase HDL and reduce LDL cholesterol, adds fiber to the digestive tract, detoxifies the body, and contains immune boosting properties.

- Cinnamon basil offers relief from diarrhea, constipation, kidney problems, coughs, headaches, and warts. It is an excellent source of a variety of key nutrients, particularly vitamin C, calcium, vitamin A, and phosphorus. Furthermore, it is a useful source of magnesium, potassium, and iron.

- Dill helps with digestion, cancer prevention (monoterpenes), dysentery, insomnia, diarrhea, and respiratory disorders. It also has anti-congestive and histaminic properties.

- Lemon balm eases pain from cold sores and herpes and offers headache relief. Its sedative properties soothe nervousness from anxiety, improve the memory, alleviate menstruation discomfort, and clear up acne.

- Mint and lemon mint helps prevent cancer (it contains a phytonutrient called perilly alcohol). It also soothes the digestive tract, and its antifungal properties are thought to play a role in the treatment of asthma and other allergy conditions.

- Oregano offers relief from diarrhea, constipation, kidney problems, coughs, headaches, and warts. It is an excellent source for a variety of key nutrients, particularly vitamin C, vitamin A, calcium, and phosphorus. Furthermore, it is a useful source of magnesium, potassium, and iron.

Different herbs set out to dry.

Fire (Heat)

Fire (Heat)

Fire is a chemical process that is a rapid, persistent chemical change that releases heat and light and is accompanied by flame. Basically it's an exothermic oxidation of a combustible substance. A much simpler definition of fire is burning fuel or other material.

Because of its characteristics of heat and light, fire is a prepper's best friend. Not only does fire provide and support all aspects of the Survival Triangle©, it also supplies the warmth necessary to regulate body temperature. It helps to keep us dry in many if not most circumstances. Fire provides light, allowing us to see near and far. Fire allows us to heat and cook food and can keep flying insects and other animals away. Fire can be used to signal your location for emergency help. It can be used to make charcoal, which can be used to cook or heat. Fire can provide a means of water purification. It can also be used for medicinal purposes, such as cauterizing wounds. The smoke from a fire can even be used to drive bees from a hive or preserve meat. Fire is a means to burn wood to make bowls, spoons, and a dugout canoe. You can now see why I consider fire my number one resource for any prepper in a SHTF or SLAE scenario.

In order to create a fire, there are three requirements: fuel, oxygen, and an ignition source. Without any one of the three items, there will be no fire. For example, without matches (ignition source) you can't start a fire. Without wood (fuel) you can't start a fire or keep it going throughout the night. And by throwing dirt on a fire you deprive it of oxygen, therefore extinguishing the fire.

Fire Triangle (courtesy of http://coachmunro.com)

Heat (fire) has a direct impact on many things, including the human body, food supplies, and water stores. The most important aspect of heat is its effect on the human body. The body regulates its temperature (98.6° F) to keep all its systems functioning correctly.

The balance between body fluids and warmth is both critical and fragile.

If you live in the northern, Midwestern, or eastern portion of the United States, heat is essential. Without heat, pipes freeze, water freezes, hypothermia sets in, and your life becomes extremely miserable. Heat sources can be fixed or portable. Fixed heat sources can include wood stoves, propane tanks, natural gas heaters, geothermal, and electric sources. Examples of portable heat sources include the Yukon M1950, the Big Buddy™, and kerosene heaters.

In a SLAE or SHTF scenario, electricity may be a luxury. This is obviously a problem if your house's primary source for cooking and heating is electrical. For example, if your stove is electric how would you cook meals for your family? The answer is easy. You need to have multiple backup sources. Backup fuel sources for cooking could include resources such as wood, kerosene, home heating fuel, propane, diesel, and even jet fuel. I previously described several of my backup heating sources but because they can be used for cooking it's worth discussing in more detail; in addition, I explain why I chose them.

Take, for instance, the Yukon M1950 stove. US soldiers in the Korean War used this stove, and it can now be purchased in military surplus stores for approximately $170. It is extremely compact when not in use, yet it assembles to provide a fully functional source of heat. This stove can use many types of fuel, including wood, jet fuel, diesel fuel, and unleaded gasoline. The entire unit weighs only twenty-eight pounds. I can easily pick it up and carry it anywhere, or use it in the house if I need to. It is perfect for both sheltering-in-place and bugging out. In addition it provides heat and the surface can be used for cooking.

Yukon M- 1950

The Big Buddy™ is a good example of a propane source that can further your redundancy. Mr. Heater's Big Buddy™ can use propane cylinders in a variety of sizes, including the one-pound cylinders you can buy at

Walmart™ or Target™. The Big Buddy™ can also accommodate larger twenty-pound cylinders. The propane cylinders connect on each side of the Big Buddy™ (inside the door) and provide ample heating times. I've used the Big Buddy™ for some time now, and I like the compactness as well as the BTUs. The Big Buddy™ has a built-in blower that can circulate heated air for heating efficiency when used indoors. The fan operates on either four D-size batteries or a six-volt A/C adapter. From a safety perspective, the Big Buddy™ has a low-oxygen shut-off system, tip-over shut-off system, and a heavy-duty safety guard. Though harder to use for cooking it can easily be adapted and used as a stove.

A third form of cooking and heating redundancy that I use is a kerosene heater. There are two types of kerosene heaters: convection and radiant. Both types have circular fiberglass wicks that use capillary action to transport the kerosene straight to the burner. In a radiant kerosene heater, the burner is in a glass cylinder that has repellent stainless steel behind it. When you turn on the device, the burner turns red and sends heat waves outward. Radiant kerosene heaters produce some convection heat, but they mostly project the heat forward, to the walls and windows. Convection is simply the movement of the air around the kerosene heater due to a temperature increase. Kerosene can last up to five years if properly stored in approved metal or plastic containers. K-1 kerosene is safe because it burns cleanly, and if you have the wick set properly, it gives off little or no smoke. The kerosene heater is economical in terms of fuel cost. In the Midwest, kerosene heaters run anywhere from fifty dollars to two hundred dollars. If there were no electricity and I had to shelter-in-place, my kerosene heater would provide light and heat. It would also serve as a stove top. To cook I would simply place my cooking container on top of the wire cage surrounding the kerosene heater. Point is that any time you have to shelter-in-place you need to be creative with the resources you have available.

Shelter

Shelter

A shelter is your primary living location, while a bug-out location is a house, underground shelter, fifth-wheel trailer, camper, cave, or other place/location that you can use in a SHTF situation; basically, it's a secondary living location. Not all individuals have access to or can afford a BOL.

Should you need to Get out of Dodge (GOOD) a BOL should be available when you need it. The BOL should be stocked with provisions and located within a few hours' drive. It takes more than five hours to drive to my BOL, which means it's not quickly accessible. As such, I have to be prepared at all times with plenty of gas, food, and other supplies.

A BOL does not have to be secluded, such as in the middle of a forest, but it needs to provide and support the elements of The Survival Triangle©. Regardless of its location, your shelter or BOL needs to protect you and your family from rain, snow, wind, sun, rodents, and insects. In addition, it needs to be able to maintain a comfortable temperature as efficiently as possible. My BOL is in the northern part of the United States. It is situated on a major lake and is surrounded by forest. We have access to fish, deer, geese, rabbits, and other wildlife. The lake can be used for our water source should our well fail. We have multiple means of filtering the lake water to provide clean, healthy water. For shelter we have an older home that is well insulated and situated fifty feet from the lake. The lot is big enough to allow a 500-square-foot garden that would provide fresh vegetables and fruits for canning in the summertime. There is easy access to the forest (within fifty feet) and an almost limitless amount of fuel (i.e., trees). The trees could also be used for building or maintaining structures such as hunting blinds. I wanted a BOL that was fairly close to a major city (approximately one hour away), yet somewhat isolated. This setting works for me but may not work for you. Your BOL could be as simple as grabbing your tent(s) and other supplies and heading to a familiar location that you feel is far enough away from the chaos. A BOL does not have to be elaborate, but it has to provide the safety you would require in a short- or long-term SHTF situation.

Without shelter and heat (fire), you won't survive a harsh winter, regardless of food, water, or self-preservation. Shelter keeps you warm in cold weather and dry in the rain. Your shelter also protects your preparations and provides psychological comfort (think "home sweet home"). Your shelter is a place where you can rest your body while providing protection from threats created by natural and man-made events.

When you shelter-in-place you need to ensure that you prepare your shelter for multiple types of events. Examples of events that you may want to prepare for include tornado, hurricane, chemical/nuclear release, pandemic (such as avian or bird flu), drought conditions, wildfire, terrorism (9/11, Boston Marathon incident), economic collapse, and temporary loss of the power grid (electricity, water, sewer). Each event will have similar Survival Triangle© elements such as food, water, and heat, but because each event is unique there needs to be different considerations. For example, living close to a nuclear power plant may require you to purchase iodine tablets or a nuclear/biological/chemical (NBC) suit.

A side note, if you live or work within ten miles of a nuclear power plant, states will provide iodine tablets at no cost.

Living in a hurricane area will require that you have boards pre-cut for windows and doors. Living next to a fertilizer plant may require that you have a gas mask to protect against ammonium nitrate. The chemical compound ammonium nitrate is an explosive chemical produced by fertilizer plants that can cause life-threatening injuries when ignited. The following is a list of recommendations you may have to take or prepare prior to sheltering-in-place:

- Close all window shades, blinds, or curtains.
- Close and lock all doors.
- Keep sheets of pre-cut plastic which can be taped around the doors, windows, and heating ventilation and air conditioning (HVAC) units to limit circulation in your shelter.
    - As an additive measure, use duct tape around all door, window, and HVAC openings.
- Create a checklist outlining procedures that should take place once you have sheltered-in-place.
- Pre-cut boards to fit window and door frames.
- Ensure all food, water, heat, communication, and protection tools and/or supplies are properly stored and ready for use.

Self-preservation (Protection)

Self-Preservation

Self-preservation is:

- the preservation of your being from harm, danger, or fear and is an instinctive tendency.
- a natural or instinctive tendency to act so as to preserve one's own existence.
- a behavior that ensures the survival of an organism; it is universal among living organisms.
- protection of oneself from harm or destruction.

Self-preservation can be both a controlled and uncontrolled action and reaction. An uncontrolled action or reaction would be when your body instinctively reacts by removing your hand from a hot stove. Before you can think your body removes the source of pain. Your body, without your input, then begins the healing process. When you have fear, your body releases adrenaline to give you increased strength and a heightened awareness to sight, smell, and hearing. This is an uncontrolled reaction. Other uncontrolled self-preservation reaction or actions include: protection (your natural instinct to protect yourself and family), navigation, psychology of self, and being able to physically defend yourself.

Controlled self-preservation actions start with proper planning. These are actions you control and plan for. As you do advanced planning to shelter-in-place you may decide to purchase weapons and store ammunition for protection. Your reaction is to purchase the weapon(s) and ammunition.

Being mentally and physically fit is a critical component of self-preservation and was previously discussed in the Second Tenet of prepping. Yet another aspect of physical preparedness is protection of the human body; a.k.a. security, self-defense, and weapons.

Without protection, and assuming you had to shelter-in-place for an extended period of time, your food, water, heat, and shelter are in jeopardy. The reason is simple. People will react differently in a SLAE. First and foremost people will always look out for themselves and their families. More to the point, people will not act as they did prior to the event, and this will include the relationships they had with other peers, families, groups, and so on. If you have to shelter-in-place for extended periods of time, say two weeks, neighbors and friends will probably run out of food and water due to a lack of preparation. They will do whatever they can to find these resources, obtaining it by any means within their power — up to and including violence. Be mentally and physically ready to protect yourself and family. My preparations include food for others outside of my family. Once that food is gone, there is no more. The remaining food will only be made available to my immediate family.

It's also critical to remember that not all preppers are truly prepared; each one has a different goal for, and understanding of, prepping. For example, some preppers may only purchase weapons and ammunition. When exposed to a SHTF scenario, they will quickly learn that they're in trouble because they lack food, water, heat, and potentially shelter. They will discover that without these elements they have failed. These preppers are smart enough to realize that there are other preppers who are properly and completely prepared. They will seek out these individuals, either in a positive or negative manner, and seek assistance. For that reason, you need protection such as firearms.

For those who have had limited exposure to firearms, it's important to provide a high-level overview of the types and classifications available. As we all know, firearms come in various sizes, models, prices, and types. In this handbook we will discuss two types of firearms: long guns and pistols.

Shotguns and rifles are the most common types of long guns. Long guns can be lever action (e.g., Walther Lever Action), pump action (e.g., Winchester Model 6), semiautomatic action (e.g., DPMS Oracle Semi-Automatic 308), hinge action, or bolt action (e.g., Winchester Model 59).

Semiautomatics and revolvers are the most common types of pistols. Pistols are classified as single action, double action, or semiautomatic, as seen in the following:

- Single action. The hammer must be cocked with the thumb prior to releasing the trigger. Most single action models require that the hammer must be cocked each and every time the gun is fired. An example is the Beretta Stampede.
- Double action. The trigger cocks and releases the hammer when released. There are two main ways that double action works. The first way is actually single action, whereby the hammer is cocked with the thumb and when the trigger is pulled, the hammer is tripped. The second way is true double action, whereby you simply pull the trigger, which cocks the hammer, revolves the cylinder, and trips the hammer, thus firing the

round. An example is the Ruger Super Redhawk Alaskan.

- Semiautomatic: A single chamber is positioned at the rear of the barrel. A slide moves backward, ejecting the fired case and then pulling another cartridge up from the magazine as it moves forward. An example is the CZ75 Omega.

I recommend having a combination of close-range weapons, long-range weapons, varmint weapons, and weapons that have a wide shot pattern when fired. In a SHTF situation, especially during the early stages, it is unlikely that you'll have a close encounter requiring firearms. Nevertheless, always be prepared. Your goal will be to keep others as far away from your main shelter or BOL as possible. This will be accomplished with your long-range arms. As time progresses and the situation becomes more desperate, you may be faced with a close encounter with an individual or a group. You need to be prepared and to understand that these people are desperate, hungry, and willing to do whatever it takes to fulfill the basic requirements of life.

From a cost perspective, buying different types and calibers of weapons can be expensive. To keep it simple I recommend the purchase of several shotguns; two at a minimum. Shotguns give you the widest shot pattern and target area for close quarter confrontations. In addition, the cost of a shotgun is significantly cheaper than rifles and handguns and the ammunition is much more readily available. I have several shotguns and to keep ammunition cost down, I buy the 100-round value packs at Walmart™ for around twenty-five dollars. As you decide which brand of shotgun to purchase I would suggest that you purchase two of the same model. This is for several reasons. First, the operation of each shotgun will be the same. Second, each shotgun will use the same ammunition and therefore not require different caliber types. And third, the parts from one shotgun can be used to repair the other. Because this subject is both controversial and personal, I will leave it to you, the reader, to determine the best option(s).

Other types of protection include tools for detecting any source of danger that may approach your shelter or BOL. You need to be alerted as soon as possible to any danger, day or night. Some tools that provide this capability are briefly described in the following:

- Infrared detectors:
  o For example, the MURS Alert Transmitter, which offers the ability to monitor activity at remote locations. The MURS Alert Transmitter utilizes passive infrared sensor

technology that will transmit an alert signal to the MURS Base and Hand Held radio in order to notify you that someone has entered a monitored area.

- o Offer real-time alerts.
- o Are relatively inexpensive to implement and extremely practical.
- o Can be placed around the perimeter of your BOL for added security.
- o Can be easily concealed, thereby avoiding detection.

- Motion detectors
  - o Can be strategically placed to detect motion.
  - o Are cost-effective and provide real-time detection.
  - o Most common motion detectors measure body heat (passive).

- Infrared (IR) game cameras
  - o Allow images to be seen in low levels of light, approaching total darkness.
  - o Do not provide real-time feedback.
  - o Take photos of images and store them to an internal disk. The disk must be manually reviewed for content.

- Closed-circuit television (CCTV)
  - o Use video cameras to transmit a signal to a specific place, on a predefined set of monitors, and therefore provide real-time observations.
  - o Can be extremely expensive, and unless you plan for its purchase, may not be practical
  - o Can purchase cameras with remote monitoring. With this option you can monitor your shelter anywhere there is a computer connection.

- Hand-held infrared video recorders
  - o Provide the capability to see heat signatures (sources) in the dark and therefore provide real-time observations.
  - o Are manually operated; therefore you have to be actively using the recorders to see the heat signatures.
  - o Are moderately expensive but practical.

- Night-vision goggles (NVGs)
  - o Allow images to be seen in levels of light approaching total darkness.
  - o Can be hands free, depending on type.
  - o Offer real-time observations.

- o Manually operated, and therefore you have to be awake.
- o Moderately expensive but practical.

- Binoculars
  - o Same as night-vision goggles but are limited to daylight use only, unless the IR option is purchased.
  - o Allow you to monitor your property, hunt, or scout from a distance.
  - o Are available in many magnifications.
  - o Price ranges vary, depending on your budget.

Experience

Experience

Experience, as modeled by The Survival Triangle©, is composed of two parts: the experience you have and the experience you need. Ideally you will have experience in all aspects within The Survival Triangle©, even as limited as it may be. This is not realistic, so you must realize what your weaknesses are. For example, if you've never shot a gun, you'll find it difficult in a SHTF situation to protect your shelter or family members; you'll blindly aim and hope for the best. If you don't have experience cooking the food you store, you won't know how to cook it at all, let alone cook it to taste. If you've never learned to repair a shelter or use alternative heat sources, you could be in for some long, cold nights. I have a phrase that I always use: "It was an experience I didn't have, but it was a skill I needed, so I went ahead and did it." You need to always have this mentality.

You should share your experience and knowledge, whether it is a specific technique or simple recommendation, to provide understanding, counsel, and guidance to others. You must also seek out others who are willing to teach new skills. Sharing the knowledge of your strengths and improving upon your weaknesses will help you become a well-rounded prepper.

So you may ask yourself, "Why do I need to share, learn, and be open-minded?" The answer is it's possible that traditional tools and methods may not work or, at a minimum, be less effective. For example, many prepper colleagues I know have their entire prepper library on technologies such as e-readers. The e-reader is a great way to store libraries of books and files, but what happens when there is no electricity for one day, two weeks, or six months? Yes, your e-reader will still be available for hours and maybe days if you have a generator. But what do you do when the e-reader no longer works? Where do you find your survival books? *Experience* and *knowledge* would dictate that it makes "common sense" that you remain open to having hard copies of books in your library. But do you?

The point is that as a prepper you have to have the experience and understanding of what resources you have at your immediate disposal and how those resources can help you and your family in a SHTF. In addition, you must be able to use them effectively, in ways they have never been used, or in ways they weren't meant to be used. Here's yet another instance: How many individuals or families would know or understand how to turn an aluminum water bottle into an alcohol stove? An alcohol stove could save your life or that of your family by providing light and heat for comfort and cooking. This is an example of a traditional tool (water storage) used for a non-traditional means (stove). In all cases you must learn, share, and remain open-minded. Having physical preparations is different than knowing how to use them.

It's not enough to read about how to do things; you need to have hands-on experience as well. My mantra is, "It was an experience I didn't have but I knew it was a Skill I needed so I went ahead and did it."

Energy

Energy

Energy is required throughout The Survival Triangle©. When I talk about energy, I do not necessarily mean electricity — although electricity greatly simplifies several components of the Survival Triangle©. I'm referring to alternative energy sources. Examples of alternative energy sources include wood, propane, batteries, steam, generators, wind, and hydroelectric technology. In order to minimize stress while sheltering-in-place, we need to prepare and have ready multiple energy sources.

Solar

Solar generators

A solar-power generator is made up of a few small components that include a battery charger, the generator itself, and the frames. The solar-panel frames on the generator gather and harness the sun's energy and store the energy in a battery. Most solar generators can store that energy for a very long time, up to a year. The smaller camping versions of solar-power generators are very lightweight and easy to assemble, so they can be moved and taken anywhere. Their portability is a large reason why they are becoming so popular among the public. Prices start around $1,200.

Solar panels -portable and fixed

<u>Portable</u> solar-power systems are similar to devices such as battery chargers, backup power generators, and even mobile devices used for wireless system work. These devices are ideal for anyone who travels and is constantly on the go. Different systems provide varying watts to power items like laptops, radios, shortwave radios, and portable lighting. Prices range from below $100 to thousands of dollars.

<u>Fixed</u> solar panels are typically photovoltaic (PV) modules or panels. The module or panel is an assembly of photovoltaic cells or solar cells. These systems are flexible enough to provide electricity for anything from a camper to a commercial application. A single solar panel will provide only a limited amount of energy; therefore, it may be necessary to purchase or install several panels to meet your energy requirements. Other components that may be required include an inverter and a battery with the appropriate wiring. These systems are based on your energy requirements, so prices vary.

<u>Wind</u>

Wind power is the conversion of wind energy into a useful form of energy, such as wind turbines that make electricity, windmills for mechanical power, wind pumps for water pumping or drainage, and sails that propel ships. Wind power, as an alternative to fossil fuels, is plentiful, renewable, widely distributed, and clean. It produces no greenhouse gas emissions. Typical wind-power units are not portable and must be installed to a fixed base. Prices range from about forty-five dollars for a thirty-two watt wind turbine to well over $100,000 for a residential system.

Hydro (Water)

Hydropower systems use the energy in flowing water to produce electricity or mechanical energy. Although there are several ways to harness moving water to produce energy, run-of-the-river systems, which do not require large storage reservoirs, are often used for micro-hydropower systems. Hydropower systems require property that has access to flowing water. Most home units utilize micro-hydro turbines connected to an alternator or similar system to produce power. These systems can be pricey, but the payoff is a green technology with the potential of producing unlimited energy.

Geothermal

Geothermal energy uses heat from the interior of the earth. This heat, or thermal energy, originates from the formation of the planet, from the radioactive decay of minerals, and from volcanic activity. Geothermal power is cost-effective, reliable, sustainable, and environmentally friendly, but it has historically been limited to areas near tectonic-plate boundaries. Geothermal systems range in price, starting at $25,000 and going up from there.

Wood

Wood is probably humankind's very first source of energy. Today it still is the single most important source of renewable energy, providing over nine percent of the global primary-energy supply (*Nations*, 2011). Wood energy is as important as all other renewable energy sources together. As previously mentioned, wood is a great source of fuel for a fixed or portable wood stove. Depending on your resourcefulness, wood can range from free to thousands of dollars, based on your consumption and type of use.

Propane

Propane is a byproduct of the production of gasoline and the refining of crude oil. Propane has been used as a fuel since 1912, and it is the third most common fuel in the United States today after gasoline and diesel. Most of the propane used in the United States is produced domestically.

Propane gas is an excellent fuel for running emergency generators. It is clean burning and readily available for delivery in many areas. Since propane gas is stored in a separate tank on-site, generators using it are usually not affected by the elements or by the types of mechanical disruptions that cause most residential power outages. For these reasons, manufacturers of emergency generators usually provide the option of using propane as a secondary fuel source. Propane generators are located outside the premises and are on standby mode until needed. When a homeowner is already using propane gas for heating or cooking, adding a propane-powered electric generator is always a good idea. Either gasoline or diesel fuel, as shipped from the manufacturer, powers most portable generators. You may convert gasoline and diesel generators to propane, thereby providing the option of two sources of fuel. You will need to consult the manufacturer of your generator before attempting any conversion.

Batteries

Storage batteries are the essential component of any independent power system. They store energy in addition to becoming a source of energy for use at a later time. They are extremely valuable when traditional (electric) or non-traditional (solar, wind, geothermal, etc.) energy sources are not available. It's critical that you choose the right battery for the right application.

These batteries could stand alone or form a battery bank that allows for longer output and the ability to support additional items that require electrical power. Here are some things to remember when considering batteries for use as an energy source in a SHTF situation:

- Battery storage has relatively high efficiency, as high as ninety percent or better. Be aware that the higher the efficiency, the higher the cost of the battery.
- Rechargeable batteries can be used as a rapid-response storage medium.
- Many off-the-grid domestic power systems rely on battery storage. Batteries designed for use in residential solar-electric systems are heavy-duty batteries designed to be discharged slowly and deeply. Typically, they range from two to twelve volts each, and a single battery can weigh up to several hundred pounds.
- There are basically three types of batteries recommended for alternative energy systems:
  o Flooded-type batteries are lead-acid batteries that can release hydrogen. Hydrogen is an extremely flammable gas, and as such the batteries must be vented if used inside.

- o Gel batteries are sealed; therefore there is no release of hydrogen.
- o Absorbed Glass Mat (AGM) batteries are leakproof and spillproof. In addition, they do not release hydrogen and are highly recommended for alternative energy systems.

Petroleum

Petroleum is a term used to describe hydrocarbons, which primarily include oil and natural gas. Examples of refined (processed) hydrocarbons include gas, kerosene, and home heating fuel. In everyday life, these resources are routinely available, but in a SHTF situation they become scarce and highly sought after. As such, your preps must include a predetermined amount of petroleum fuels, based on your needs. We store twenty gallons of kerosene (heater), sixty gallons of diesel (truck), thirty-five gallons of unleaded (generator and car), and ten gallons of white fuel (cooking or fuel lanterns). Below are more details:

Gasoline

Gas is a volatile, flammable liquid made from petroleum and used as fuel in internal-combustion engines. For the prepper, this will be the most common short-term fuel used. I say short-term because in a SHTF situation, there may come a time when gas is no longer available. You will need to store a sufficient quantity of gasoline to run any gas-powered cars, generators, or other applications.

Diesel

Diesel is any fuel used in diesel engines. Home heating oil or fuel oil is nearly the same as diesel. Home heating oil contains red dye to distinguish it from the diesel you buy at a gas station. The reason is that taxes are lower on home heating fuel than on diesel fuel used for cars and trucks.

Caution: *Although you can run home heating fuel in your diesel engines, **do not do it**. If you get caught, there are severe penalties.*

Kerosene

Kerosene is a must for preppers. Its applications include heaters, cooking stoves, and oil or kerosene lamps (e.g., Aladdin lamps). Kerosene is much safer to use than gasoline, natural gas, or propane. It can be purchased from your local fuel supplier, some gas stations, and hardware stores. I recommend storing enough kerosene to support your applications (heater, lamps, etc.) for a minimum of three months.

Medical Bug Out Bag (MBOB)

Other Considerations

Medical Supplies

Although they are not specifically mentioned in The Survival Triangle©, medical knowledge and supplies are critical when sheltering-in-place. Obtaining medical knowledge could be as simple as taking a CPR or first aid course, or arranging for access to a medically knowledgeable resource such as EMTs, nurses, physician assistants, or even doctors. Medical resources also include books and guides that explain how to deal with specific circumstances in an emergency. In addition, it's important to have the proper basic medical supplies on hand. There may be many medical concerns while sheltering-in-place, but you won't be able to cover them all. Being prepared for the basics will help. Always have a Medical Bug-out Bag (MBOB). This is not to be confused with a Bug-out Bag (BOB), which contains personal items such as clothes, bug-out gear, and so on.

An MBOB will contain emergency supplies and resources (see list below) that will be useful should an emergency situation arise. An MBOB should contain at least one to two months' supply of any medication you're taking. If you have to shelter-in-place for multiple weeks it may become extremely difficult to get refills or new prescriptions. For example, my son is asthmatic and as such we have at least two months' supply of inhalers on hand at any one time.

Basic medical supplies should give you the capability to treat minor to serious issues. Given the vast array of medical possibilities, you're not going to be able to store everything. Store the essentials, which include but are no means limited, to the following:

- Abdominal/pressure pad
- Ace bandages
- Adhesive bandages (assorted sizes and types)
- Alcohol (both fifty percent and ninety-one percent by volume)
- Alcohol wipes/antiseptic
- Antibiotic ointment (stock up on this)
- Betadine
- Burn Gel (a two percent lidocaine-based salve)
- Celox (stops bleeding in as little as thirty seconds)
- Emergency cash (small bills)
- Feminine hygiene products
- First aid references (handbooks, pamphlets, etc.)
- Gauze (assorted sizes and types)
- Hydrogen peroxide
- Ibuprofen/acetaminophen/Imodium/Benadryl/ Zyrtec or similar drugs

- Instant cold/hot packs
- Iodine wipes and/or swabs
- Liquid Skin or similar substance
- NIOSH-certified N95 Mask (filters out H1N1)
- Personal medications
- Printed material (books, pamphlets, guides, etc.)
- Splinter-removal kit
- Sting-relief wipes
- Super glue
- Tape, scissors, latex gloves, tweezers, and thermometer
- Tourniquet
- Wound-care kit with various sutures

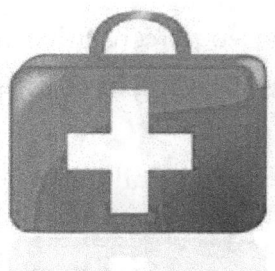

Communications

Communications

When sheltering-in-place you should have multiple communication platforms available. Having the latest information will keep you informed of the current conditions and future plans. These tools will help determine when it's no longer necessary to shelter-in-place and if any additional actions should be taken. Below are examples of some useful communication devices and their characteristics:

- Emergency dynamo radio - This is a great radio to have as many brands can operate from a battery, electricity, or dynamo. When batteries or electricity are not available, the radio works via the dynamo. The dynamo is charged by cranking a handle in circular motions which charges an internal battery.

- Shortwave radios - Shortwave radios can receive radio transmissions on frequencies between three and thirty MHz, which enables worldwide communications and the ability to stay informed. In addition, shortwave radios can be heard from thousands of miles away and are extremely economical to purchase. Shortwave radios can operate off of a 12-volt car battery.

- Cell phones – A great, portable option. However, there have been many events in which cell phones have been useless. During 9/11 cellular service requirements were so overwhelming that very few calls were completed.

- Land lines – An alternative to a cell phone. There are times when a land line is available and cell phones aren't.

- Internet – Assuming it's available

- MURS (Multi-Use Radio Service) - MURS are two-way radios with a limited transmitter-power output of two watts. The radios are capable of transmitting three to four miles based on line-of-sight and one to two miles with minimal blockage from buildings or trees. MURS are economical to purchase and practical as they transmit and receive on frequencies relatively unknown to the general population. MURS are battery operated.

- CB radios (Citizen Band radios) - CB radios can transmit no farther than 155 miles per FCC regulations, but in practice, they transmit no more than four to twenty miles based on line-of-sight. They are economical to purchase and would be a great addition when sheltering-in-place. Operates off of a 12-volt battery.

- GMRS (General Mobile Radio Service) - GMRS radios require a valid GMRS license to operate. The license is issued through the Federal Communications Commission (FCC) but nevertheless is my preferred method of communication. They are FM/UHF radios that operate at short distances only. There is significantly less radio traffic on GMRS radios as compared to walkie-talkies purchased from the big box retailers. This is a huge advantage in any SLAE or SHTF. They are moderately priced. GMRS radios are battery operated.

General Mobile Radio Stations (GMRS)

- Ham radio (amateur radio) - Ham radios require a license and transmit on frequency modulation (FM) and single sideband (SSB). Ham radios receive and transmit throughout the world and are moderately to high-priced. Ham radios are highly recommended when sheltering-in-place as they have the ability to operate from a 12-volt battery.

- Television – Assuming electricity is available.

As a side note, you must also be careful with your communications. Sixty-foot antennas can be seen from a distance and let others know your location. It's best to use antennas that are strung from tree to tree or at lower levels. Keep in mind that people will be monitoring the airwaves for any type of communication. They can easily determine if your communications are short-range or long-range communications. Transmit as little as possible. You do not want to reveal your location.

Lighting

Lighting

The focus of this section will be portable lighting as required when sheltering-in-place. Portable lighting is used whenever your primary light sources are not available. For example, in a rainstorm the power goes out and you need light. One would typically light an oil lamp or bring out the flashlights. These are examples of portable lighting in that they are easily accessible and lightweight. Furthermore, they produce sufficient lumens (a measure of the total "amount" of visible light emitted by a source), and they can travel with you wherever you need to go. Below are examples of lighting options and their characteristics. Examples include:

- Flashlights, headlamps, lanterns, and fluorescent strips - The majority use standard batteries. The cost is relatively inexpensive, dependent on brand, and they can provide redundant lighting sources for family members (i.e., more than one light source). These types of lights vary in lumens and weight for portability.
    - o Standardize on one type of battery for all your flashlights. For example, I highly recommend AAA-size batteries as they can be used in flashlights and headlamps.

LED Flashlight

- Outdoor solar lights - Solar lights are recharged by the sun via a solar panel. They have several advantages, such as using a renewable energy source (i.e., the sun) and can be easily found at any local hardware store. In addition to being portable they are inexpensive, ranging from four dollars to sixty dollars. Bring them indoors at night when you need the light and set them out during the day to recharge.

- Light sticks - Light sticks are easy to store and use. They have a short life span of one to sixteen hours. If you chose to purchase light sticks, I recommend buying in small bulk units on eBay, Amazon or other sources. I prefer the yellow-colored light sticks.

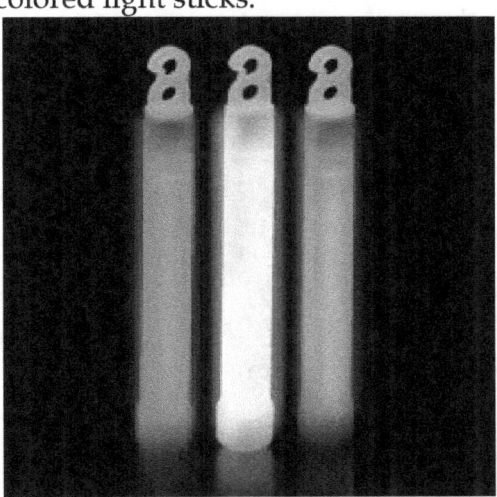

Light Sticks

- Candles - I highly recommend honey candles over wax perfumed candles. Candles are portable but do present a fire hazard due to the open flame.

- Dynamo flashlights/lanterns - Dynamo flashlight/lanterns use the Faraday principle of electromagnetic energy to eliminate the need for batteries. Basically, by cranking a handle energy is created and then stored in rechargeable battery cells. This stored energy is used to power the bulb. As the flashlight is used, it has to be recharged (cranked) to provide sufficient lighting.

- Kerosene lamps - Kerosene lamps come in many forms including Aladdin lamps. The amount of heat, which directly impacts how much light is produced, is adjusted by a wick. They are easily transported from location to location but do present a fire hazard if tipped over.
  - o Aladdin lamps – Similar to oil lamps but use kerosene as the fuel source. Aladdin lamps are considerably brighter than oil lamps

- White fuel lanterns – White fuel lanterns are available from many manufacturers, with the most recognizable being Coleman™. The fuel is easily purchased at local retailers, and I highly recommend buying extra mantels, glass globes, and pumps. White fuel lanterns are portable and reasonably priced, but they are a fire hazard if used inappropriately.

- LEDs (Light Emitting Diodes) - LEDs come in various types, from large lanterns to those worn on your head or body. LEDs can operate on everything from 12-volt battery banks to AAA-size batteries. Most portable LEDs worn on the head or body operate off of AAA-size or AA-size batteries.

- Propane lanterns - Typical propane lanterns use one-pound propane cylinders that are sold at local retailers (e.g., Target™, Walmart™, etc.). They are easy to use, convenient, portable, and cost-effective. Once again, they pose a fire hazard if used inappropriately.

- Oil lamps - Oil lamps operate off of lamp oil (i.e., liquid petroleum). The amount of light desired is adjusted by raising the wick up or down. Oil lamps are both portable and cost-effective. They pose a fire hazard if used inappropriately.

Be aware that walking around outdoors with flashlights allows others to identify your position and therefore compromises your location. Indoor lighting does the same but also lets people know that you may have some form of electricity. One recommendation is to make blackout curtains or shades for the windows for your primary shelter or BOL.

Everyday Carry (EDC)

Everyday Carry (EDC)

Everyday carry items are tools you keep with you at all times, regardless of where you go. These items could save your life or the lives of others at a moment's notice. EDC items are cleverly concealed, or in a few instances exposed, on your body. They may be worn around your neck. They may be on your belt or hidden inside the waistband of your pants. EDC items can be hidden around the liner of your baseball cap or under your shirt. They can be strapped to your leg or hidden under a long-sleeved shirt. There are many ways to conceal most items.

It's up to you to decide what items you will carry. Your EDC items will change based on where you're going and what you're doing. For example, you would not carry the same EDC items on a business trip as you would on a hunting trip. While a knife or blade is extremely useful for field dressing a deer, the Transportation Security Administration (TSA) would never allow knives or any type of blade on an airliner. It's important to know your surroundings and what EDC items are useful and appropriate. Examples of EDC items that you may choose to carry include the following:

- Flashlight
  - Your EDC flashlight must be compact in size and bright enough to illuminate your target. For weight reasons it should use AA-size or preferably AAA-size batteries.
  - One good choice, the Streamlight© Stylus Pro, is slightly larger than a pen and puts out forty-eight lumens of light.
- Leatherman© or a similar multi-tool
- USB (flash drive)
  - Use this to store and gain access to data. In everyday life a USB drive is practical and sometimes necessary. In a SHTF, and assuming there is no power, a USB will not do you a whole lot of good.
- Pocket notebook
- Pen
  - Some manufacturers make pens that double as self-protection devices or flashlights.
- Folding knife
- Firearm
  - Be sure to follow state laws for carrying weapons.
- Paracord (a.k.a. parachute cord)
  - This can be worn as a bracelet, but I don't recommend it. You need to minimize the amount of attention you bring to yourself. An

easier way is to replace your shoestrings with paracord or simply carry about thirty feet of paracord in your pocket.

- Lighter
  - o Keep it simple and buy a disposable lighter.
- Thin wallet for carrying only the basics
- Piano wire
  - o This can easily be hidden within the brim of your hat.
- Pepper spray
  - o This useful item quickly disables any attacker.

Bug-Out-Vehicle (BOV)

Bug-Out-Vehicle (BOV)

How will you and your family get to your bug-out location (BOL)? For this you need a bug-out vehicle (BOV). In some instances families have multiple BOVs due to work locations, travel plans, and so on. My BOL is five hours away, so preparation is extremely important.

Here are several questions to ask when selecting a BOV:

- First and foremost, what can you afford?

    o Be reasonable here. Odds are you're not going to purchase that $50,000 top-of-the-line truck. When I purchased my truck, I bought an older model that has reasonable mileage and works just fine. If I could not pay cash for a vehicle, then I would not buy it.

- What type of engine are you looking for (i.e., gasoline, diesel, electric or hybrid)?

- What types of fuel would you like your engine to use?

    o For example, diesel engines can burn multiple types of fuel, including home heating fuel, biodiesel, and vegetable oil.

- Do you want or need four-wheel drive?
  - o Four-wheel drive gives you the ability to go off-road, either in an emergency or to get to your BOL.

- How much fuel should your BOV be able to carry?
  - o Remember, not only do you need enough fuel to get to your BOL, you will need extra fuel due to its potential lack of availability in a SHTF situation. You must assume that gas stations will not have gas or diesel fuel readily available. This is for several reasons. The number one reason is that everyone will panic and quickly realize they need gas because they're not prepared for the situation at hand. Lines will form and tempers will flare. The second reason is that if the power goes out, the gas pumps will not work anyway. As mentioned previously, I personally observed this during 9/11. Consider the following:
    - o Is there room to install an external fuel tank in the vehicle?
    - o Is there room to carry extra gas cans?

- How much storage space do you need in your BOV?
  - Do you need the storage capacity of a truck or will an SUV or smaller vehicle have enough space?

- How many passengers do you expect to carry?

- What body style do you want for your BOV? Consider these options:
  - A truck includes a cab for passengers (if desired) along with a cargo bed. It may be used to haul large, heavy loads and can have four-wheel drive.
  - Most sport utility vehicles (SUVs) have a higher carrying capacity than cars. They have up to three rows for passengers and can have four-wheel drive.
  - A sedan typically has four doors, seating for five or six people, and a trunk for storage. Sedans come in many sizes.
  - A van is a box-shaped vehicle that often has sliding side doors. Vans typically have higher clearance than cars (they sit higher off the ground).

- o   A wagon is a four-door vehicle with an open cargo area at the back and a rear lift-gate. Wagons can typically seat five or six people.
- o   A crossover is a combination of an SUV and a sedan, often without four-wheel drive.

My BOV is a Dodge truck 4X4 that runs on diesel and it has the quad cab. I wanted a truck for the cargo space. Though it is a short bed, I can carry an abundant amount of supplies, or I can put a camper shell on it and use it for shelter. I liked the diesel engine for its torque. We had a fifth wheel, and we found that as we traveled through the mountains of the western United States we needed torque. The quad cab allows the family to drive in comfort and minimizes the kids fighting with one another. I have an in-bed sixty-nine-gallon diesel gas tank. In addition, I have a reinforced steel rack that I put in the receiver hitch on the truck which allows me to carry an additional thirty to thirty-five gallons of diesel fuel. In total I can carry about 130 gallons of diesel. This gives me plenty of gas to get to my BOL and still have plenty left over. The 4X4 provides some peace of mind because I know that if I need to go off-road to get to my BOL, I could. Finally, the diesel engine allows me to use alternative fuels and not have to rely on one type (like a gasoline engine). I can burn home heating oil, vegetable oil, biodiesel, and with a lubricating agent, some kerosene. In a SHTF situation I want the flexibility to know I can use multiple fuels due to the fact that diesel may not be available.

It's critical to have spare parts for your BOV and to know how to remove and install them. Essential spare parts may include starters, alternators, fuel pumps, filters, hoses, oil, and brakes. Once again, the idea is to be prepared before you have to be prepared.

But-Out Directions

Bug-Out Directions (BODs)

The next thing to consider is how you will navigate to your BOL. It may sound easy enough to grab your GPS and head to the nearest major highway — but that would be a mistake. In a SHTF situation, major highways will be crowded with people all trying to do the same thing: get out of town. These major highways will be the only route that the majority of people know. When cars run out of gas, the highways will become death traps. People will panic, and even more cars will block the highways.

Now you probably see the need to plan your escape route. You should have at least two escape routes that use back roads. First, plan a route that uses secondary roads and avoids major highways. Second, create an additional route that uses tertiary roads. You may be traveling the back roads of America, but the outcome will be to arrive safely at your BOL. You can simply handwrite each route or you can highlight a map. Either way, the goal is to provide clear, easy-to-read directions to your BOL.

You must assume that your GPS will not work. This could be the case for several reasons. First of all, satellites may be unavailable or shut down. Second, solar flares, which induce geomagnetic storms, travel at the speed of light and affect GPS receivers, typically beginning one hour after eruption. Third, coronal mass ejections, which induce geomagnetic storms and reach the earth one to three days after eruption, have the threat level of solar events. And finally, there is jamming, which is an intentional act by a person, entity, or country to block and confuse the GPS receiver. GPS receivers are extremely sensitive and therefore easy to jam.

If your bug-out location is within the United States, your bug-out directions should include an atlas and maps of any counties or states through which you plan to travel. I suggest you photocopy your bug-out route and then laminate it for protection. You should create copies of your BODs and place them in each BOV. In addition, I highly recommend that you identify your escape routes by using highlighters on the map itself. Use a different color to mark each route. At night and during times of stress, the highlighted portion of the map will provide contrast relative to the background of the map. The goal is to make it easy to see and easy to navigate. Once again, make copies of the highlighted map, laminate them, and place a copy in each BOV.

I highly encourage you to drive each of your emergency routes to get a better sense of what you might encounter while bugging out. While driving each route, observe your surroundings and mark the following on your map or BODs:

- Major landmarks
- Sources of water
- Safe places to rest if you need them
- The time it takes to get to your BOL
- The number of vehicles you pass on your way (You don't want your route to be too crowded with people or cars.)
- Grocery stores and gas stations
- Local law-enforcement offices
- The types of roads you're driving on (e.g., two-lane or country roads)

Finally, make sure there are no major obstacles on your escape route that would prohibit you from reaching your BOL. For example, let's assume that you need to get to the Upper Peninsula of Michigan from elsewhere in the state. You should not create a route that includes traveling over the Mackinac Bridge because the bridge could be damaged or closed to traffic. Why take that chance? Although an alternative route may increase your driving time to the Upper Peninsula, you can be assured that you will arrive at your destination without problems.

Couponing

Couponing

You may wonder why couponing is included in this book. The reason is simple: Most people who decide to prepare become overwhelmed at the cost. The first thing to remember is that you don't have to buy everything at once. As previously mentioned, Prepping is an ongoing adventure that will last your lifetime. If you're like me, you will constantly find items to add to your preperations and they don't have to be expensive or name brand.

In the following pages I describe ways to use coupons to increase your stores. I focus on food and household goods, as those offer the biggest bang for the buck in the couponing world. First of all, you and your family need to determine your level of brand loyalty. Do you buy only one brand of soup or cereal or are you open to other brands (including generics)? The more flexible you are, the more choices you will have. Keep in mind that brand name items typically cost more and they are not always on sale when compared to store and generic brands. In addition, I've found that certain name brand coupons are almost impossible to find and rarely if at all on sale. From here on, I'll assume you're open to different brands, you've purchased and tried several store and generic labels, and you liked them. Now, it's time to find some coupons.

The first place to start is the Sunday newspaper. There you'll find three sources of coupon books: Red Plum, Proctor & Gamble (P&G), and Smart Source. These coupon books are not in the Sunday paper every week. A great website that tells which coupon books will be in your Sunday paper is www.sundaycouponpreview.com. This site offers a service that will send you an email, about midweek, describing which coupon books will be available that Sunday.

Many coupons are also available online. Websites to check include the following:

- Coupons.com
- Smartsource.com
- Redplum.com

You can also download coupons directly from vendor websites. You typically have to sign up with an email address and agree to occasionally receive marketing information.

There are also websites that sell coupons in bulk. You simply select the coupons you need and pay a small fee.

The fee is based on the number of coupons, the value of the coupon savings, small administrative charges, and shipping costs. This may sound like a lot of money, but it really isn't. For example, let's say you want to buy ten Old Spice deodorant coupons that are for one dollar off the product. The fee might be calculated as follows: 10 coupons X $.10 (10 percent of the $1.00 coupon face value) + $.50 (administrative fee) + $.75 (shipping fee) = $2.25. The administrative fee is charged only once per order, so if you purchased other coupons along with your Old Spice deodorant coupons the administrative fee for your order would still be just fifty cents. Two examples of these coupon-clipping services are Couponclippers.com and Thecouponmaster.com.

It's important to shop at grocery stores that double your coupons. Doubling of your coupons simply means that if you use a fifty-cent coupon the store will double its value, making it worth one dollar. I've never seen grocery store double coupons beyond a one-dollar coupon value. When we first started couponing there were no grocery stores in our area that doubled coupons, so we had to travel forty-five minutes to reach one. The gas almost cost more than the savings, but the trip still made financial sense.

We soon learned that some of the best deals could be found at stores other than grocery stores. Drugstores like Walgreens and CVS had stellar deals for our needs. These stores run great sales on necessities like toothpaste, deodorant, feminine products, school supplies, first aid supplies, cereal, and other household items. We purchase items when they're on sale and when reward cash or similar incentives are offered. Reward cash is basically a coupon that the store gives out for use at a later time. For example, suppose that Crest toothpaste is on sale for two dollars with one dollar in reward cash. We buy the toothpaste for two dollars, use a one-dollar coupon, and receive one dollar in reward cash. This essentially makes the toothpaste free!

The math looks like this:
$2.00 Crest – $1.00 coupon – $1.00 reward cash = $1.00 due at time of purchase, with a $1.00 reward cash to use at the next visit.

Many stores have BOGO (buy one get one) sales. Sometimes the item is BOGOF (buy one get one free), and sometimes it's BOGO half off. When you purchase two items as part of a BOGO sale, most stores still allow you to use two manufacturer coupons (one per item) — and you can use your reward cash, too! Keep in mind that each store has separate policies on couponing and the easiest way to learn them is to ask for the store policy. Stores may also offer some type of customer-loyalty discount card. I recommend signing up for these, as you can use them to save money on food and in some cases fuel. Stores such as Kroger allow you to load coupons on the card directly from their website and then redeem them at checkout. This beats having to carry around 200 paper coupons.

In couponing you have to be patient. The item you need or want will not always be on sale, nor will there always be a coupon for that item. Coupons are seasonal, meaning that the coupons you find in October will not be the same as those you find in November. Most coupons do expire, so keep track of their dates — but don't feel like you have to use every one. Don't buy an item with a coupon if it's not something you want or need.

Remember the following: Buy what you eat and eat what you buy.

Staying organized is the tough part. With hundreds of coupons, where do you put them all? We chose a simple system that uses index cards and plastic note card holders. We purchased five of these holders and labeled them Hygiene, Dairy, Groceries, First Aid, and Household. We then labeled the index cards by the brand and category of the item. For example, coupons for Crest toothpaste go in the "Hygiene" index card box behind the card labeled "Crest." I like things to be quick and easy, so this works for me. There are more formal systems out there. Some people use binders, while others use shoeboxes. Your goal is to find a system that works for you.

Couponing was the tool that allowed us to begin Prepping. It allowed us to purchase not only food but also first aid and household items to put in our Prepping storage at a reduced or reasonable price. We still use coupons today, but we only buy what we'll use. We are not the type of people who purchase 200 of one item simply because we have coupons and we can. We are also free to share with others what we have learned. As the Third Tenet of Prepping discusses, you need to reach out and help others when you can, before they reach out to you.

Sheltering-In-Place (SIP)

Sheltering-in-Place

As previously defined, sheltering-in-place is an emergency procedure for individuals, groups or organizations whereby you seek protection and cover by remaining at your current location, residence or alternate location.

The reason you prepare, using The Survival Triangle© as a model, is because in a SHTF or SLAE you will be sheltering-in-place to minimize exposure to danger and maximize survival.

More often than not, families will shelter-in-place at their 'primary shelter.' A primary shelter is a residence you rely on for protection and comfort. This is most often where you live on a day to day basis such as a house, trailer, apartment or condominium.

Your goal as a prepper is to safely shelter-in-place knowing you have prepared to the best of your ability! The timing of when to shelter-in-place is based on the event or the availability of information to suggest your life or safety is in danger. Due to the unpredictable nature of when you may have to shelter-in-place, it's vital that you understand all elements of The Survival Triangle©.

When to Shelter-in-Place

It's critical to shelter-in-place anytime you have knowledge or a concern that external events could or will affect the safety of you, your family, group or organization. This decision should be based on the most reliable information available at the time. There may even be times when you're ordered to shelter-in-place by law enforcement or government officials.

There are two broad categories of events that trigger when you shelter-in-place: natural and man-made events.

Natural events often require that we shelter-in-place, but in many cases we are given advanced notice such as the Nor'easter of February 2013:

> *"A massive storm packing hurricane-force winds and blizzard conditions **is sweeping through the Northeast**, dumping nearly 2 feet of snow on New England and knocking out power to more than a half a million customers.*
>
> *More than 23 inches of snow had fallen in parts of central Connecticut by early Saturday, and more than 21 inches covered Randolph in southeastern Massachusetts..."* (Lindsay, 2013).

At other times Mother Nature gives us a warning that a significant life-altering event may occur but doesn't tell us when. Such is the case with avian flu or bird flu, H7N9, which had not been previously found in humans:

> "Two people in China have died and another remains critical after falling ill with a strain of bird flu not detected before in humans, the official Chinese news agency Xinhua reported... A team of experts assigned by the health commission established that the three cases were human infections of H7N9 avian influenza, which has not been found in humans previously, the news agency reported... The better known H5N1 avian flu virus has infected more than 600 people since 2003, of which 371 have died, according to the WHO..." (Mullen, 2013).

Counter to Mother Nature are man-made events. Man-made events can occur at any time, are often impossible to predict, and can have a significant effect on mankind.

An example of a man-made SHTF in which an entire city had to shelter-in-place was the domestic terrorist attack at the Boston Marathon in April 2013. As National Public Radio (NPR) explains:

> "Local officials have defended the decision to essentially lock down the city of Boston on Friday

while law enforcement searched for a suspect in the Boston Marathon bombing.

Residents were told to remain indoors during the hunt for Dzhokhar Tsarnaev, who survived an early morning shootout with police in the suburb of Watertown during which his brother, Tamerlan, was killed.

Massachusetts Gov. Deval Patrick announced the decision to lock down Watertown and the surrounding areas, including Boston, at a dawn news conference Friday.

"We're asking people to shelter-in-place — in other words, to stay indoors with their doors locked and not to open the door for anyone other than a properly identified law enforcement officer," he said.

It is not unusual to lock down schools and other institutions when there are reports of gunfire. And after the Sept. 11, 2001, terrorist attacks, the nation's air traffic was halted and some other sites thought to be potential targets, such as the New York Stock Exchange, were closed. But to shut down a large part of a metropolitan area is another thing, says Frank Cilluffo, director of the Homeland Security Policy Institute at George Washington University.

"In terms of both scale and scope, the shelter-in-place that was enforced was extraordinary, perhaps even

unprecedented, but so too were the circumstances,"
Cilluffo says." (Naylor, 2013).

There was no advanced warning of this attack and as such it was nearly impossible to prevent. The outcome was devastating in that three people were killed, over 250 injured, and an entire city had to shelter-in-place.

Where to Shelter-in-Place

Where you shelter-in-place is mandated by:

- your current location (which may or may not be your primary shelter)
- distance to your primary shelter if not currently at that location
- distance to a bug-out location if your primary shelter is no longer safe
- weather
- magnitude and type of event
- availability of food, water, heat, and protection at your primary shelter or bug-out location
- timing of the SHTF or SLAE event (i.e., whether it has already occurred or if you are given advanced notice to determine where you will shelter-in-place).

Once again, you have three options: shelter-in-place where you are, travel to your primary shelter and then shelter-in-place (a.k.a. "bug in"), or bug out to a safer alternate location. An example of a situation in which you have no choice but to shelter-in-place at your current location is the Carnival Cruise Line fiasco in February and March 2013. As CNN reported:

> *"That about sums up how people are describing conditions aboard the Carnival Triumph on Tuesday as tugboats slowly drag the stricken cruise ship toward Alabama -- and freedom for its 3,143 passengers.*
>
> *Some on the ship reported sewage sloshing around in hallways, flooded rooms and trouble getting enough to eat after a fire in the ship's engine room Sunday left it drifting in the Gulf of Mexico. Passengers dragged their mattresses onto the ship's open deck to stay cool and get away from the nasty smells inside.*
>
> *"The odor is so bad, people are getting sick and they're throwing up everywhere," said Brent Nutt, whose wife is aboard the ship."* (Joe Sutton, 2013).

As can easily be deduced, these passengers had no choice but to shelter-in-place and make the best out of a dire situation.

An example of when you are given ample time to leave your current location and head to your primary shelter is, once again, the winter storm of February 2013:

> *"Blizzard conditions again descended on the midsection of the country Monday, bringing hurricane-force winds to the Texas Panhandle, closing highways in Texas and Oklahoma and putting already snow-covered parts of Kansas on high alert as the day progressed.*
>
> *National Weather Service officials issued blizzard warnings and watches in Kansas and Oklahoma through late Monday. As the storm tracks north and east across West Texas toward Oklahoma, Arkansas, Kansas, and Missouri." (Blaney, 2013).*

In this case there was absolutely no excuse why individuals or families should not have been able to shelter-in-place at their primary shelter as the weather service gave advanced notice of the storm.

An extreme example of when you may want to bug out to an alternate location that provides additional safety above and beyond that of your primary location is a nuclear event, either local or international. Dylan Stableford describes one such situation:

> *"The North Koreans need to understand if they attack an American interest or an ally of this country, they're going to pay a heavy price," Graham said on NBC's 'Meet The Press' on Sunday. "I could see a major war happening if the North Koreans overplay their hand this time, because the public in South Korea, the United States, and I think the whole region, is fed up with this guy." (Stableford, 2013).*

This is an extreme example but nevertheless can be applied to similar situations such as floods, nuclear power plant meltdown, chemical/biological attack, economic crisis, power grid failure, and many other emergencies. The decision to bug out is a personal decision based upon the information at hand, your risk tolerance, and timing.

Basic Sheltering-in-Place Guidelines

If a SHTF situation occurs, there will be a time frame where you shelter-in-place, dependent on the magnitude and effects of the event. This is why you need to be prepared. The time frame will vary based on the type of event/scenario, your provisions, the severity of the situation, your comfort level, the availability of a vehicle or bug-out location, time of the year, and so on. Sheltering-in-place not only provides security, it also allows for the emotions of the event to be processed and hopefully better understood. During the Boston Marathon domestic terrorism incident, city officials mandated that citizen's shelter-in-place. As I see it, this was for two reasons: security and emotions. Because the location of the two suspects was unknown, it was critical that officials ensure the safety of all Bostonians. This could only happen by sheltering-in-place. The mandate to shelter-in-place allowed law enforcement officials to more easily collect evidence and search for the suspected terrorist. From an emotional perspective, when the incident first occurred, information was scarce and unreliable. Emotions were extremely high as runners and bystanders were wounded and/or treating those who were wounded. Tension was high. The entire city was looking for answers and direction. By sheltering-in-place, individuals and families were allowed to reflect on what had happened and await further communication — all in a secure environment.

During the initial stage of any SHTF situation that requires sheltering-in-place, there will be confusion, lack of direction, chaos, and many unanswered questions. The population will be looking for guidance on what steps to take next, as well as information about the situation (i.e., what caused it, how long it will continue, when the electricity will be on, where to find first aid stations, how to get food, etc.). All levels of government — local, county, state, and federal — will be extremely selective about when, how, and what they communicate. When you shelter-in-place, you do not expose yourself or your loved ones to the chaos (i.e., to either the chaotic situation or other people who are not prepared).

Within hours and sometimes days of the situation, the landscape will change dramatically. Individuals and families who aren't properly prepared will begin to panic. They will begin to realize that if assistance hasn't arrived, it most likely isn't going to arrive anytime soon. Their limited food and supplies will have been consumed and the grocery and hardware stores will have nothing else available. The biggest concern will be the lack of food and water. These individuals will begin to look outside their usual sources and ask others for basic supplies. Maybe others will give, but maybe they won't. As time goes by, people will become desperate. In order to protect their loved ones and save their lives, they may do things they would never have previously done. When this stage arrives, and preferably some time before, head to your bug-out location should you have one. If you have no bug-out location or are unable to reach it, you will continue to shelter-in-place while always remaining vigilant.

Where you shelter-in-place or bug out to needs to provide you and your family the necessities of life, but remember, it won't remove the challenges that remain ahead. How well you prepared will determine the actions you take and how long you will be able to shelter-in-place.

In a long-term sheltering-in-place scenario you need to be constantly aware of the noise you produce as well as the light you use at night. There will be people out there searching for any sign of generators, guns, cars or machinery that will signal the possible presence of food, fuel, shelter, or even ammunition.

How Long to Shelter-in-Place

You shelter-in-place as long as it takes for the event or the effects of the event to be rendered safe. This is often a personal judgment call but can be aided by information from various sources. Sources can include neighbors, newspapers, television, shortwave radio, word of mouth, local/county/state/federal governments, and the internet. At times government authorities will directly indicate that it's no longer necessary to shelter-in-place.

My family is prepared to remain self-sufficient anywhere from six to twelve months. We're not preparing for a TEOTWAWKI (The End of the World as We Know It) situation. Instead, we're focused on an event such as a tornado, earthquake, hurricane, flood, economic crisis, and short-term man-made events — basically anything that would have a mass effect on society with severe repercussions. In most instances, six months should be more than enough time for electricity, food, water, and other essential services to be restored.

In conclusion, I would state that we're all aware that there is no guarantee in life, let alone in the decisions we make. But what I do know is that being properly prepared for a SHTF or SLAE can negate a negative outcome in many situations.

Should you have a continued interest in preppers or prepping and would like detailed information, see my other books available at Amazon.com. They are *The Prepper's Survival Guide: An Introduction to Prepping and a Guide to Fire*, *The Christian Prepper's Handbook*, and *A Guide to Sheltering-In-Place*. All titles are listed under the author name Zion Prepper.

I hope you found the information in *The Prepper's Handbook* valuable, and God bless the United States of America.

Bibliography

Almond, D. (2010). "WROL - Without the Rule of Law - in the here and now" (2010, June 2). Restore the Constitution. Accessed July 7. http://restoretheconstitution.wordpress.com/2010/06/02/wrol-without-the-rule-of-law-in-the-here-and-now/

Army, U. (n.d.). Emergency Drinking Water Disinfection Procedure. Retrieved October 6, 2011, from Emergency Drinking Water Disinfection Procedure: phc.amedd.army.mil/PHC%20Resource%20Library/31-008-1004.pdf

Blaney, B. (2013, February 25). 2nd blizzard in less than week slams Plains region. Retrieved April 28, 2013, from news.yahoo.com: http://news.yahoo.com/2nd-blizzard-less-week-slams-plains-region-124708575.html

Crain, J. (2007). Food Storage Shelf Life. Retrieved May 9, 2013, from Family Survival Planning: http://www.family-survival-planning.com/long-term-food-shelf-life.html

Harrison, Judy A, E. L. (2006). So Easy to Preserve (5th ed.). Athens, Georgia: Cooperative Extension Service, The University of Georgia.

Health, W. S. (2009, January). Public Health and Response. Retrieved October 6, 2011, from Purifying Household Water: http://www.doh.wa.gov/phepr/handbook/purify.htm

Lindsay, J. (2013, February 9). Huge storm blankets Northeast with 2 feet of snow. Retrieved April 28, 2013, from Yahoo News: http://news.yahoo.com/huge-storm-blankets-northeast-2-142830361.html

Mullen, J. (2013, April 1). 2 dead in China from unusual bird flu strain. Retrieved April 28, 2013, from CNN.com:

http://www.cnn.com/2013/04/01/world/asia/china-bird-flu-deaths

Naylor, B. (2013, April 22). Boston Lockdown 'Extraordinary' But Prudent, Experts Say. Retrieved April 27, 2013, from National Public Radio (NPR): http://www.npr.org/2013/04/22/178446136/boston-lockdown-extraordinary-but-prudent-experts-say

Prevention, C. f. (2006, May 27). Center for Disease Control and Prevention. Retrieved October 6, 2011, from Water Treatment Methods: http://wwwnc.cdc.gov/travel/page/water-treatment.htm

Nummer, B., B. J. (2008, September). Canned Goods. Retrieved 13 2013, June , from Utah State University Cooperative Extension: http://extension.usu.edu/foodstorage/htm/canned-goods

Stableford, D. (2013, April 7). Is North Korea on the brink of war? Retrieved April 28, 2013, from news.yahoo.com: http://news.yahoo.com/blogs/lookout/north-korea-kim-jong-un-war-201715650.html

Silverman, Sterling Dr. (2012). Chapter 5: Food. Retrieved August 4, 2013, from The New Survivalist: http://www.thenewsurvivalist.com/golden_rule_of_food_storage.html#mbp_toc_7

Sutton, J., D. A. (2013, February 12). Cruise ship still gross, passengers say, but it's finally moving. Retrieved April 28, 2013, from CNN.com: http://www.cnn.com/2013/02/12/travel/cruise-ship-fire

Wellbeing. (2012). "Physical." Washington State University: Wellbeing. Accessed July 7. http://www.wellbeing.wsu.edu/physical.aspx.